FDA at Irvine

Zimmer Gunsul Frasca Partnership

Edizioni Press
New York

FDA at Irvine
Raul A. Barreneche

The building of the U.S. Food & Drug Administration's new regional headquarters in Irvine, California, designed by Zimmer Gunsul Frasca Partnership (ZGF), is a story nearly a decade in the making. The new home for the Pacific Regional Laboratory-Southwest and Los Angeles District Office reflects a sea change in the operation of the agency (part of the Department of Health and Human Services), its image, and its architectural identity. For the architects, it represents a challenging program: a technically demanding laboratory and office building on an environmentally sensitive site, built for the U.S. government during a period of unprecedented concern for safety and security. To meet these requirements with ZGF's customary level of efficiency and design skill would be, as partner R. Doss Mabe described, a "mission impossible."

But it was a necessary mission. Until the dedication of the new building in June 2003, the FDA's regional personnel labored for decades in geographically disparate locations that made cooperation and efficiency a difficult proposition. Lab technicians were housed in a windowless 1950s building in the notorious Pico-Union neighborhood near downtown Los Angeles, one of the nation's most dangerous urban zones. Meanwhile, the district's field staff was headquartered 40 miles away in Irvine, Orange County.

The fundamental separation, both physical and psychological, between field personnel and lab staff made the agency's operations difficult. Field employees are responsible for bringing in samples of food, drugs, cosmetics, and medical devices—everything from cabbages and shellfish to condoms and sleeping pills—to be tested by the FDA in accordance with its role as a regulator of the safety and accurate labeling of these products. The laboratory staff used to analyze the samples for irregularities and illegalities was far removed from the field operatives who brought them in. In the early 1990s, the FDA decided to reorganize this regional structure, consolidating its operations in a single location to improve efficiency and reduce costs. The move also reflected the agency's desire to change its institutional culture from a closed operation shrouded in complex bureaucracy to an open, flexible, and efficient venture that embraced advances in science and technology.

In 1995, the FDA selected ZGF, in joint venture with Henningson Durham and Richardson (HDR), to give form to their vision of a streamlined, centralized regional office. The agency selected an undeveloped ten-acre site near the campus of the University of California at Irvine for its new roughly 135,000-square-foot home, which brought together the previously isolated field, lab, and administrative teams under a single roof.

The FDA's new facility adjoins the San Joaquin Freshwater Marsh Reserve, one of the few freshwater coastal wetlands on the Pacific Flyway in Southern California. ZGF's response to that site—especially to the topography and views of the preserve—was fundamental to their entire scheme. The building could hardly turn its back on the unspoiled wetlands, a surprising pocket of green within the unbridled though manicured sprawl of Irvine, itself part of the almost nonstop flow of suburban density from Los Angeles to San Diego. This marshy patch of brome grass, needlegrass, and fescue, a haven for roadrunners, mallards, hawks, and egrets, is a window onto Southern California's past, when the coastal plains extended from the mountains to the sea.

ZGF oriented the building to take advantage of these splendid views, but took the design a step further to make it part of its site. The architects delineated the building's footprint with a gesture that follows the curved contours of the land as it descends into the marshes. A canted 450-foot-long wall of 1/4-inch glass sheltering an open public space along the entire length of the building mitigates between the boxy footprints of the interior labs and the sinuous topography of the site. This internal street opens itself to the views of the marshland and fills the interiors with daylight, breaking down the apparent length of the space and regularizing the stepped profiles of the three bays of office and lab areas as it arcs back on itself. The building's massing takes the language of the curving floor plan into three dimensions: canted curves in glass and concrete and nested copper-clad vaults create a sculptural ebb and flow in synch with the site's gentle march down to the wetlands.

For a federal facility such as this, with all of its requisite privacy, security, and opacity, ZGF had limited options for physically opening up the building. In fact, the security requirements were upgraded twice during the building's multi-year design and construction: once after the 1995 bombing of the Alfred P. Murrah Federal Building in Oklahoma City, when the FDA building was in design, and again after the attacks of September 11, 2001, by which time the project was already in construction. And the distinct and intensive mechanical requirements of the lab component meant that, at best, only the administrative half of the building could contemplate a physical openness to the exterior.

The architects' strategy of a glazed double-height circulation spine framing the wetlands created a seamless connection to the outdoors. The broad, sunlit space suggests a giant, curved veranda that, if not physically, experientially opens the whole of the building to nature. It's as if an entire façade has been taken out and the movement down stairs and along the corridor extended outward. The view is surprisingly pastoral: it seems as if Irvine's office parks and shopping malls have pushed themselves aside to make room for a broad green expanse of grasses and marshlands extending all the way to the San Gabriel Mountains, 70 miles away.

This sensitivity to site and desire to integrate interior space with the outdoors builds on the tradition of the great Southern California modernists. The pioneers of the early and mid 20th century, among them Rudolf Schindler and Richard Neutra, seized on the opportunity to weave indoor and outdoor space in the region's dry, mild climate. Of course, Schindler and Neutra were able to push the intermingling of interior and exterior to extremes in their residential commissions: Witness the outdoor living room, complete with fireplace, and rooftop sleeping perches of Schindler's own landmark house on Kings Road in Los Angeles. Incorporating outdoor space into institutional buildings would always prove a more difficult matter, especially in a secure government building such as the FDA facility.

Still, ZGF tried to weave outdoor space into their design as best they could. They originally conceived the employee dining area as a café beneath the welcoming entry portico, but increased security after September 11th forced it to move indoors. They were able to keep small open-air spaces throughout the building, such as informal break areas tucked between the lab wings and the perforated copper screens enclosing the exit stairs. The long, curving glazed corridor facing the wetlands is a credible attempt to bring the outdoors in despite the mandates of keeping the building enclosed. And as the building's main gesture to the site, it succeeds.

The corridor is also the building's "main street," a busy route through which all of the building's occupants pass to reach their offices and laboratories. Three bays of offices on both levels, primarily rows of open workstations, flow unimpeded into the communal circulation path and the view beyond; the architects liken these clusters to neighborhoods, supporting the analogy of the double-height corridor as a main thoroughfare.

On the ground floor, the serene library marks the terminus of the indoor street, which originates just beyond the main lobby, between the employee lunchroom with views of the wetlands and the vaulted, copper-veiled conference center. On the second level, a suite of offices for the directors and a computer training facility mark the opposite ends of the lofty axis. The space is what contemporary theorists would espouse as a "social condenser," a magnet for activity and a cross-pollenizer of functions that animate space more than a programmatically specific room. ZGF doesn't overly theorize the concept; the simple analogy of a veranda or an internal street sufficiently captures the architects' aims.

The most original and unexpected of the building's exteriors is the entry façade. Flanking the front door is the concrete vault of the conference center, sheathed in a curving shell of perforated copper that screens a glass curtainwall and a standing seam copper roof that continues the curvature of the perforated screen. Both the form and cladding of the conference center pick up the drum-shaped volume of the adjoining stair tower. The actual entrance is sheltered by an angular portico with a canted aluminum frame that continues the curvature of the north-facing curtainwall beyond the limits of the building, and creates a spatial tension against the solid wall of the conference facility. As the initial visual impact made on visitors and employees entering the facility, this façade sets the tone for the entire building: informality and openness, but also adventurousness and innovation, just the kind of image the FDA hoped to communicate in its new facility.

The visual and spatial permeability of the curved glass façade and the corridor behind it reflect significant changes in the FDA's institutional image. ZGF's design suggests not a secretive, opaque bureaucracy, but a transparent, future-minded, and open—within limits—institution. That character comes through clearly in ZGF's architecture. The massing breaks the building down into smaller, more visibly comprehensible blocks that are easier to navigate inside. From the moment one enters the building, beneath a welcoming double-height standing-seam copper portico, it is evident that this is not a typical federal building. In fact, it's hard to imagine that unknowing passers-by would identify it as a government facility at first blush.

Even with the increased security demands on government buildings in recent years, the FDA facility remains remarkably unobtrusive. There is, of course, a black painted chain-link fence surrounding the entire site perimeter. From the street, there is little that could be done to diminish the appearance of the barrier, but along the wetlands side, tall marsh grasses should conceal the fence as they grow in, creating an invisible barrier between the building and the preserve. Also, as ZGF's architects were required to alter their original site plan to meet tighter security requirements, they moved the visitor parking area 300 feet away from the building and added bollards along the entry drive to protect the main entrance. The employee dining area was moved indoors, and a guardhouse added at the entrance to the facility. Fortunately, the FDA had the budget and wisdom to ensure that these extra security measures not appear as afterthoughts to ZGF's original scheme. The architects were able to design a poured-in-place concrete guardhouse with painted aluminum and glass, which they call their tribute to Marcel Breuer.

In his sublime Salk Institute in nearby La Jolla—for many architects the sine qua non of laboratory design in the modern area—Louis Kahn memorably staked out its connection to the natural world by means of a monumental axis of running water. That channel, reaching toward the distant horizon of the Pacific, makes a powerful gesture to nature on a grand scale. ZGF's winding glass wall, by no means as heroic as the muscular concrete volumes of the Salk Institute, also forges a strong tie to nature. The glazed façade is a broader, softer gesture that wraps the landscape with a simple, shallow curve. It forges a more intimate relationship between the laboratory and the land, between science and the natural world. The architects hydro-seeded the ground all the way up to the building with the same native grasses found in the marshes, reinforcing the close tie between architecture and landscape. This connection to the site, at the very heart of ZGF's design, is one of the building's most successful ideas.

References to Kahn are not platitudes or facile analogies between two laboratories in Southern California built four decades apart. There are palpable shades of Kahn in the skillfully detailed poured-in-place concrete work and in the effect of light on these surfaces, as in the fan-shaped first-floor library at the eastern end of the building. Here, sunlight washes down the faceted walls and warm maple bookshelves through angular skylights and glazed vertical slots that slice through the center of each of the library's six bays. The play of bright California sunlight on smooth concrete and pale wood has an unmistakable air of Kahn; the classic Danish modern pendant lamps originally designed by Poul Henningsen in 1958 also lend the space a Nordic air, though on a sunny day the light would be too bright to ever mistake the space for a Scandinavian interior.

Kahn's spirit is most evident in the fine concrete work of the laboratory wings. ZGF detailed the horizontal and vertical joints between the poured-in-place wall panels with sharp, V-shaped profiles that create thin highlights and subtle shadows on the pale, slightly reflective concrete, much as Kahn did at the Salk. Like Kahn, ZGF created additional rhythms on the solid walls by exposing the reinforcing-bar tie holes within each panel. Even at roughly $255 per square foot, slightly below the going rate for a well-built commercial laboratory, the architects were able to elevate the building far beyond its relatively modest price tag with sharp detailing that gives tough common materials a sophisticated sheen. They used slightly reflective concrete, standing seam and perforated copper, steel, and glass, materials that eschew frigid monumentality in favor of tactility and warmth.

The palette also tries to speak to the FDA's newfound desire to embrace technology in its building. This is not a high-tech building in the vein of Norman Foster or Richard Rogers—that is to say, High-Tech as a style—nor is it high-tech in its use of state-of-the-art building systems. The FDA wanted to espouse advances in science and technology, but the building lacks any major material innovation. The curving glass façade, for instance, is a straightforward curtain-wall composed of an aluminum structural grid with PPG's 1/4-inch Solexia glass, which has a slight green tint. This elevation includes glass panels with a custom-designed ceramic frit pattern to cut down on glare; since it faces north and east, there is no need for additional solar control. Although the technology of this elevation is not cutting-edge, it is very well crafted from off-the-shelf components.

On the south- and west-facing laboratory blocks, the building takes on a much different character. ZGF carefully oriented the openings in the concrete-clad laboratory blocks, which overlook the staff parking lot and access to the visitors' parking area, to ensure the lab spaces received adequate daylight without adding heat build-up and glare. The openings are a combination of narrow vertical slots interspersed within larger vertical swaths of aluminum-framed curtainwalls. These towering bands of glass, extending the full height of the building, occur at the notched corners of the serrated floor plate of the labs, and bring daylight both frontally and laterally into the hallways that access the laboratories. These south-facing openings, shaded by polished stainless steel sunscreens and bands of ceramic frit in their lower reaches, help bring daylight into the lab spaces, supplementing the natural light that permeates the interiors through the glazed north façade. The sunscreens themselves are exactingly detailed, with solid stainless steel fins at their outboard edges and corrugated, perforated stainless steel panels extending back to the edge of the building. They are, however, somewhat unresolved in the end.

The separation into three distinct volumes lets the labs maintain efficiently boxy floor plans while following the curvature of the glass office façade and, by extension, the site's topography. The external stair towers, clad in curving, pleated skins of perforated copper sheeting, introduce a non-orthogonal geometry to these elevations and help break up the rectilinear nature of the lab blocks, as do the curving copper roofs shielding the extensive mechanical equipment above the laboratories.

The lab and entry exteriors get to the true character of ZGF's design. This is not the sleek buttoned-down modernism typical of recent high-profile courthouses and federal buildings designed by the likes of Richard Meier and Thom Mayne of Morphosis. Rather, it's an energetic ensemble of elemental blocks clothed in simple, fairly brusque materials. The choice seems appropriate for a roll-up-your-shirtsleeves facility where workers go about the messy business of sampling produce, pills, and medical devices. It's not a building for the public, or one with a grand civic or ceremonial connotation. This facility has much more workaday functions: testing fish for salmonella and examining heads of lettuce for pesticides. Beyond the building's unglamorous but important function, the informality of these exteriors speaks to a contemporary Southern California tradition of celebrating humble or tough industrial materials in buildings of a more exalted status. Until Frank Gehry elevated titanium and stainless steel and even chain-link fencing to new aesthetic heights, they were the materials of industry, not artistry. In this context, ZGF's choice of perforated copper screens and standing seam metal roofs seems an appropriate one. However, despite the skillful Kahnian concrete work, these elevations obscure the building's plan.

Inside, the building reflects the FDA's mission to create a pleasant, flexible, and efficient workplace. User-friendliness manifests itself in the low partitions of workstations that allow natural light to reach deep within the floor plate and colorful components in the cubicles that enliven the open office areas. The adjoining laboratories also boast colorful accent walls and lively floor patterns. As Mabe suggests, these touches of color bring energy, vitality, and "emotional content" to what could otherwise have remained sterile, white-on-white labs. The proximity between these labs and the field staff workstations, another physical embodiment of the FDA's emphasis on a streamlined, cooperative work environment, simplifies interaction between agents and technicians just a few feet away. The practical goal of such an arrangement, unique among similar FDA facilities, is increased efficiency in the process of inspection and analysis, and lower operational costs. The agency also hopes that the closeness among teams of technicians and field personnel in various specialties will inspire productive, multidisciplinary collaboration that could not have occurred under the previous system of geographically disparate offices.

The design of the lab wings reveals more than just perceptual openness and transparency. ZGF and laboratory planners Earl Walls Associates designed the concrete-frame lab blocks as mechanically, climatically, and even structurally independent of the office spaces, which are framed in steel. The blocks, each covering about 20,000 square feet, are slightly skewed from one another in plan, but maintain a rational, regular footprint. The residual corridors between the blocks contain shared support and core functions including bathrooms, elevators, electrical closets, and photocopy areas; separate but conjoined corridors wrapping the back side of the lab zones, behind the concrete façades, bring daylight into the labs through vertical glazed slots and bands of aluminum-framed floor-to-ceiling curtainwalls. The perimeter hallways also access the loading dock and four exit-stair towers shielded by gauzy veils of corrugated, perforated copper. These are considered materials handling and service corridors that provide secure access to lab areas.

The labs within each zone are highly specialized according to the particular substances being tested. The labs on the lower level are generally partitioned into smaller cells. The westernmost bay houses medical devices, instrumentation, and entomology labs; the center bay houses sample prep space and an organoleptic lab, where trained scientists smell seafood, mostly shrimp, to determine possible contamination; and the eastern block contains a lab for pesticide chemistry analysis. The upper level areas, dedicated to drug chemistry, food chemistry, and microbiology, are wide open spaces—the scientific version of a lofty art studio. This loft-like feeling gives the precision-driven work of scientists and technicians a more creative cachet. Though specialized, the labs provide as much flexibility as possible: benches and lab tables are fitted with wheels which allow them to be moved around easily, to access utilities and test equipment as needed.

The complex mechanical systems that feed laterally into the laboratory spaces extend the full length of the perimeter corridors and remain exposed above the hallways. The 17-foot floor-to-floor height for each of the two laboratory levels ensures enough vertical space for the miles of cables, pipes, and especially large ventilation ducts required for the building's current requirements, and, more importantly, space for unforeseen additions or replacements. As Mabe explains, most changes to existing laboratories occur with respect to mechanical systems. ZGF's strategy of accommodating building systems beneath tall ceilings, as opposed to creating separate interstitial spaces between floors, makes the process of layering in additional utility lines or mechanical equipment—or changing them altogether—a straightforward task. Their location alongside the labs also minimizes disruptions to the operations during maintenance and construction.

Just as the moveable lab equipment affords a degree of day-to-day or short-term flexibility, the mechanical plan gives the entire facility a level of long-term adaptability. The client's needs and functions may change in the future; technology will surely evolve to make today's systems inefficient, if not obsolete. The ability to make such adaptations without significantly altering the building is an important accomplishment of ZGF's design. Even if the systems or operations change, the rest of what works well in the building—the adjacency between labs and offices, the abundant natural light supplied to both types of work spaces—and the fundamental parti remain valid. This, too, is one of the great successes of ZGF's scheme.

ZGF has designed numerous labs for clients in private industry; creating a similar facility for the FDA involved considerations that may not seem apparent. Laboratories for pharmaceutical companies or biotechnology firms tend to be designed in accordance with the vagaries of real estate markets and business plans. They are conceived with a shorter lifespan; they can even be considered disposable, for instance, with an inexpensive tilt-up concrete structure. The FDA building, by comparison, is meant to last much longer: 50 to 100 years without major structural changes. But because the mechanical systems can only be expected to last less than half that amount of time, ZGF's strategy of easily changeable systems ensures that technology can keep up with a structure built to last.

ZGF handily achieves clarity and functionality with its plan and its bright, flexible interiors, but it is difficult to translate from two dimensions into three. However, when measured by the energy and enthusiasm with which the FDA and its staff have taken to their new home, ZGF's design is a resounding success and bodes well for the government's continued embrace of modernism in federal buildings. Regardless of any perceived architectural shortcomings, the FDA building's openness, humanity, informality, and adventurous modern design spirit are among its most important contributions. That it managed to achieve these goals while meeting the complex demands of a secure federal building combining offices and state-of-the-art labs on the edge of a protected wetland is no small feat. It has taken many years, but ZGF's "mission impossible" is now mission accomplished.

The shape of the building is a direct response to its site, overlooking a protected wetland sanctuary at the head of Upper Newport Bay. It arcs gently along an elevated ridge at the sanctuary's southwestern edge. This situation affords both close intimate views down to the adjacent marsh, and majestic distant views to Saddleback Peak and the San Gabriel Mountains. Entry to the site is from the west, near the north end of the building, while parking is kept to the south and west, well away from the principal views. Because of its curved shape, its length, and its relatively low profile, the building embraces and captures the extensive open space of the sanctuary as if its own site were limitless. This embrace is reinforced to a greater degree by bringing the native wetland landscape directly up to the base of the curved glass wall facing it, thus obscuring the boundary of the site.

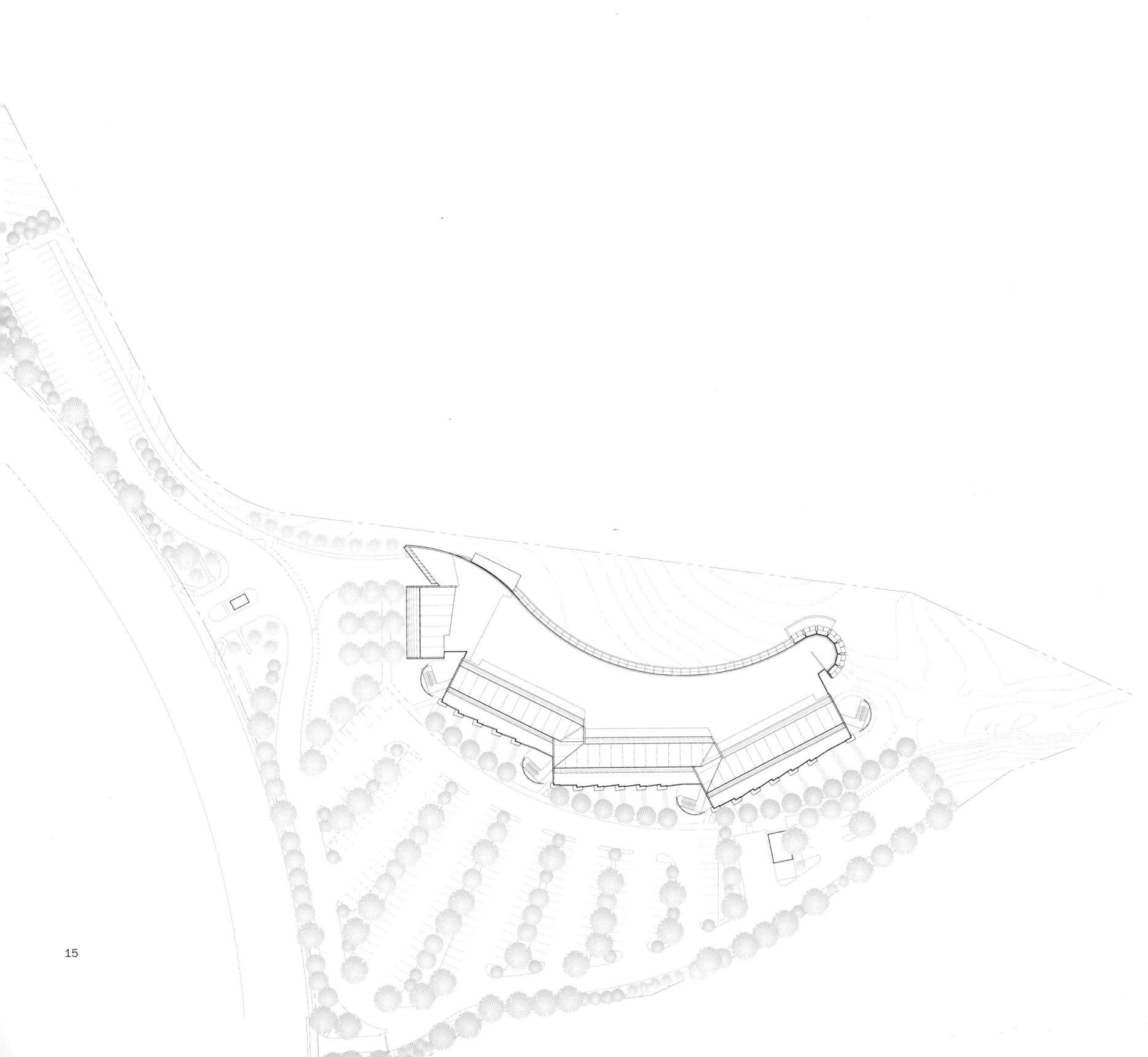

Complex intersections between curved and orthogonal geometries dictated the careful locating of the building's structural elements during design in order to facilitate the construction process.

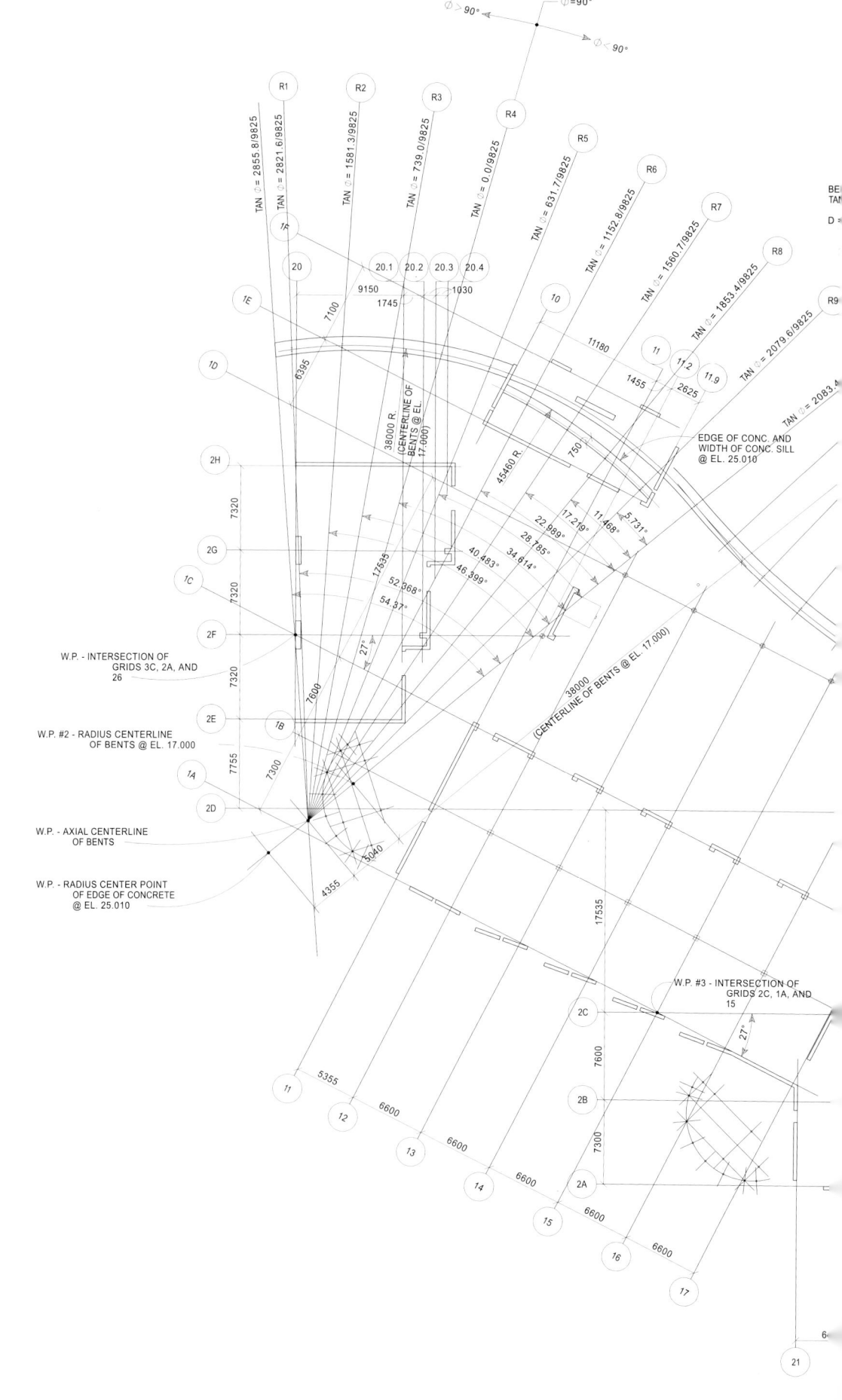

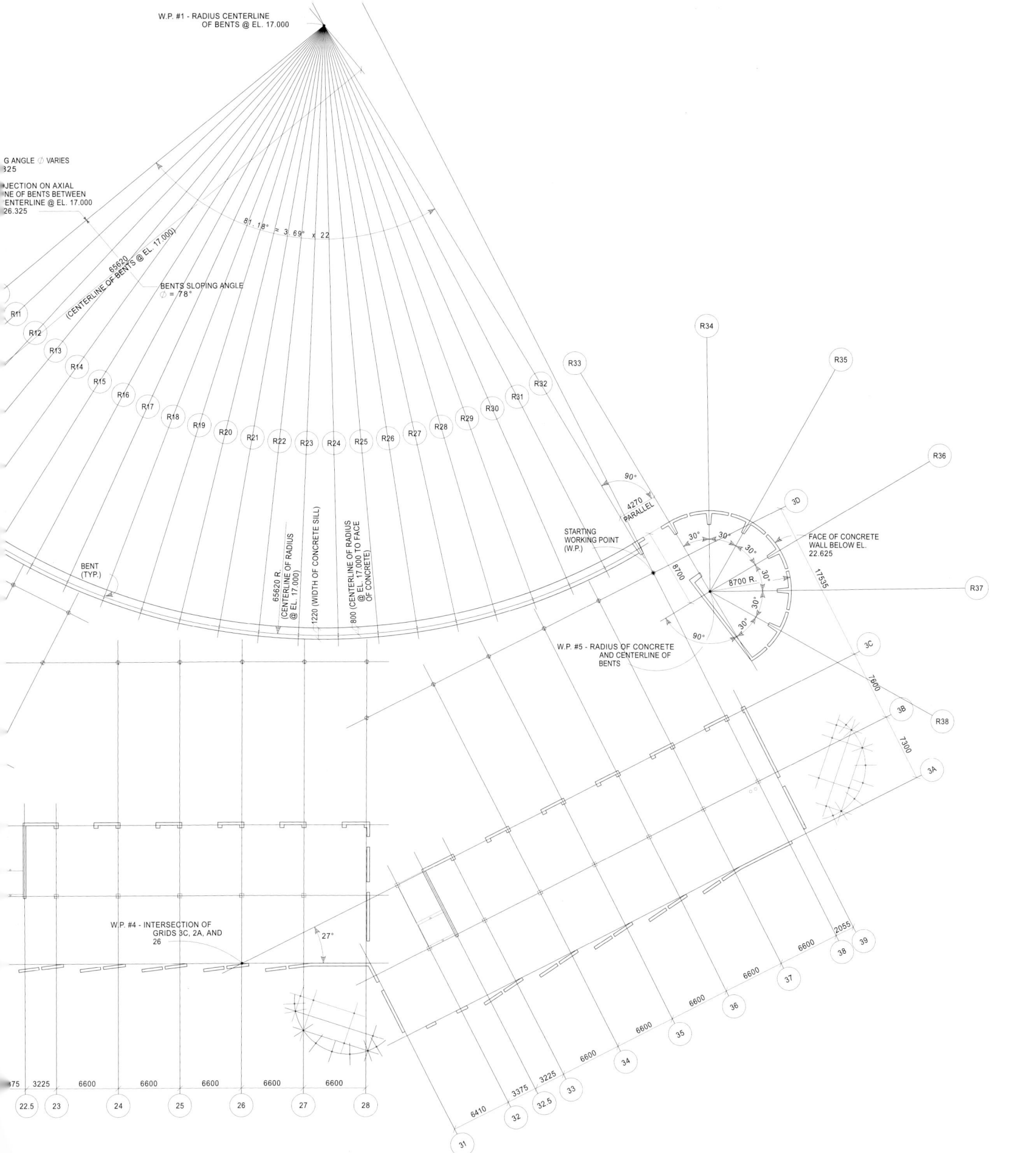

A typical cross-section through offices and laboratories reveals the inherent rationality of an extremely economical response to both program and structural and service elements.

Site considerations are married closely with the strict functional requirements of the program in the geometry of the building's plan. Three two-story rectangular laboratory blocks, each consisting of 11 identical modules, are arranged in a stepped echelon facing southwest on the site. They are constructed of relatively heavy cast-in-place concrete slabs, supported on concrete columns and enclosed by thick walls that provide required lateral stability for the whole structure. Within these rationalized concrete boxes, complete flexibility is provided for the laboratories. To house the office components of the program, a light steel structure is attached directly to the concrete walls of the laboratories behind the curved glass wall which faces northeast. Against this sloped wall, and overlooked by the upper level office mezzanine, is a curved two-story space punctuated by three open stairs. This main, public circulation route through the building is complemented by two adjacent staff aisles at the intersection of the laboratories and offices. At the opposite side of the laboratories lies the main service corridor with open access to mechanical, electrical, data, and plumbing systems. Shared conference, dining, and library facilities are located at each end of the public circulation space.

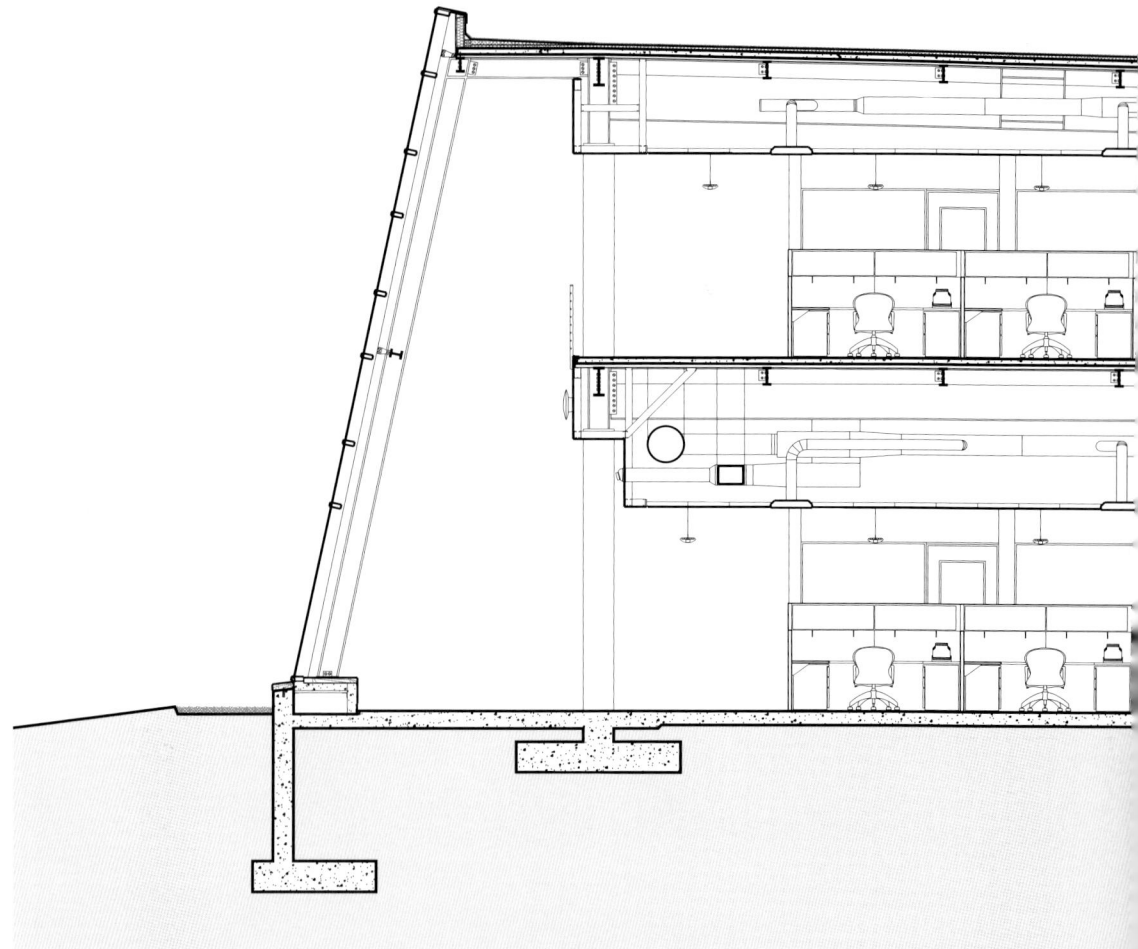

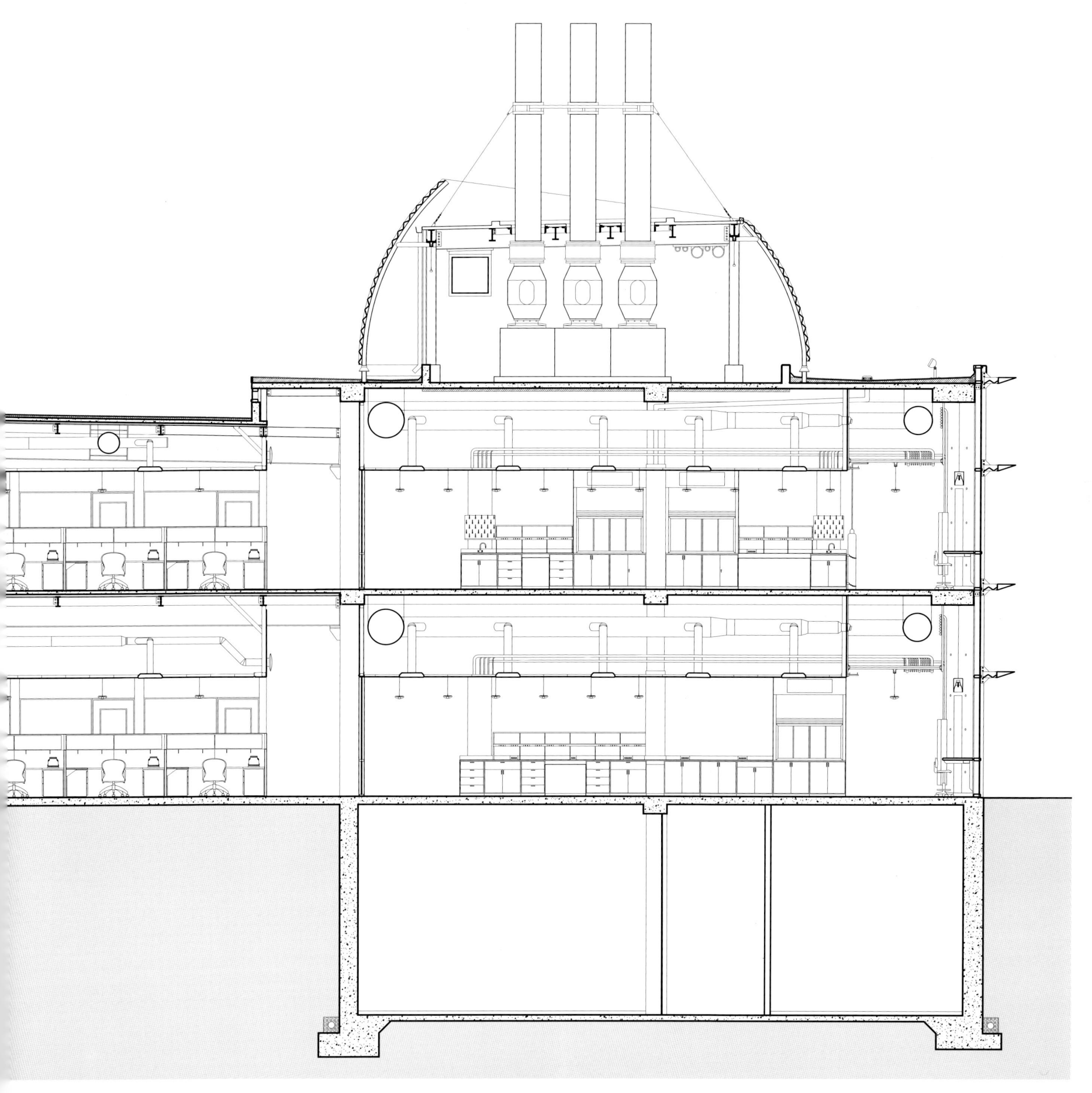

Viewed from the wetland sanctuary, the building displays a romantic aspect that belies the rationality of the plan and section. This façade, below the perforated copper penthouse screen, is anchored by the concrete masses of the library, the dining pavilion, and the conference center.

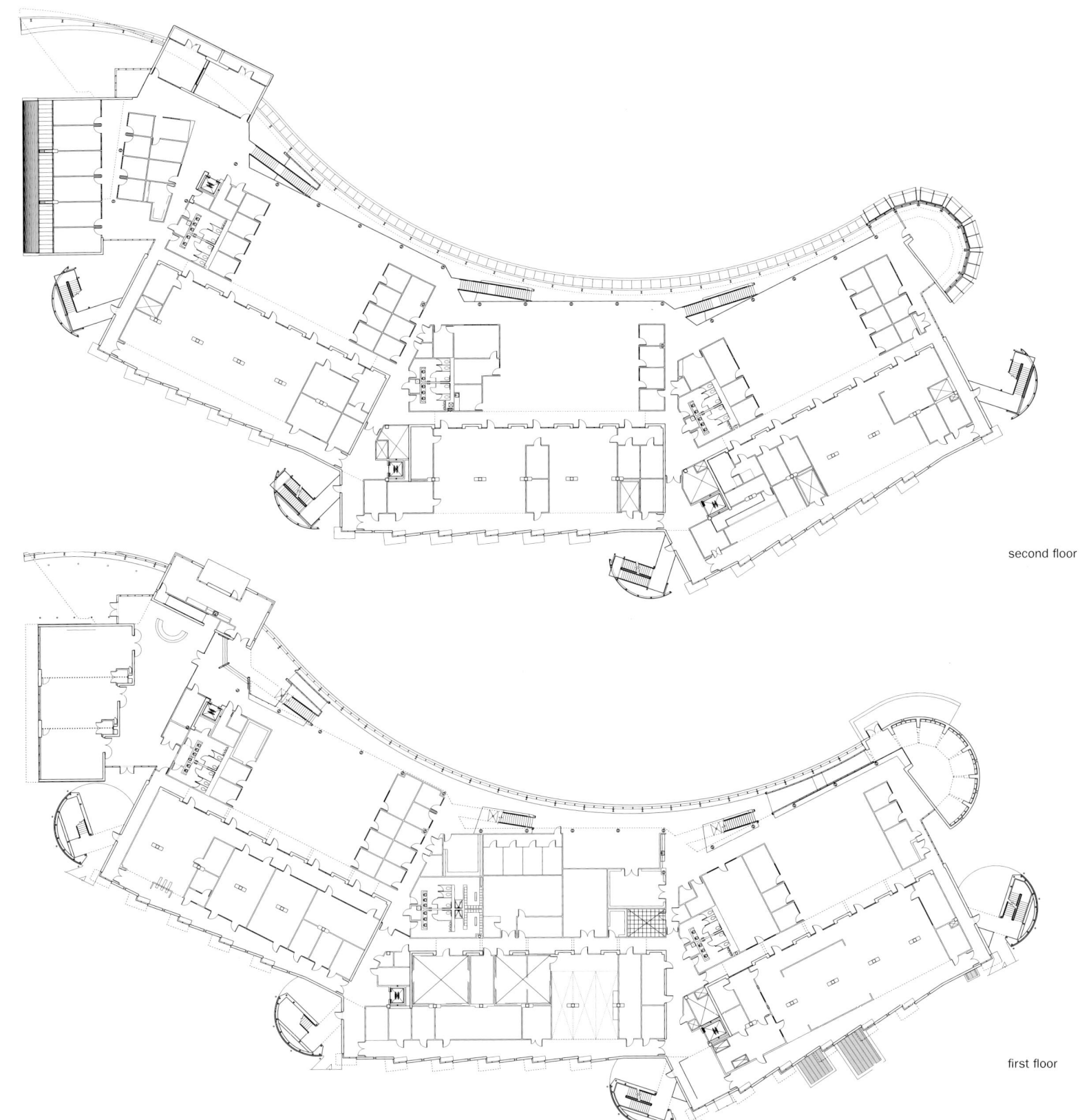

second floor

first floor

Reached from the entrance lobby and stretching through to the library at its far end, the two-story public circulation space is conceived as a curved internal street with access to every area of the building. Flanked by a sloped full-height wall of glass along its length, it opens directly on its opposite side into open-plan office neighborhoods. The sweep of the curve obscures its actual length of over 300 feet. As one moves along, one perceives it as a vertical chasm of space that affords an unexpected sense of intimacy and immediacy to the view of the wetlands beyond. It is conceived in the classical California tradition of a space that is in-between—uniting inside with outside—and rendered highly transparent through the extensive use of glass. The ceiling of the offices is held back to the mezzanine floor-line to emphasize the lightness and continuity of the steel structure overhead with painted steel bents that support the glass wall.

During the day, the sloped glass wall reflects the sky, and its planar surface is relatively mute.

OVERLEAF: At night, lit from within, the building becomes a transparent object that can be seen from a great distance across the open landscape.

Despite its sinuous arc, the glass wall is detailed with stock aluminum sections. All glass is flat and the vertical modules of the wall are almost entirely repetitive. Aluminum glazing sections are clipped to the edge of the roof deck and to horizontal struts spanning between steel bents.

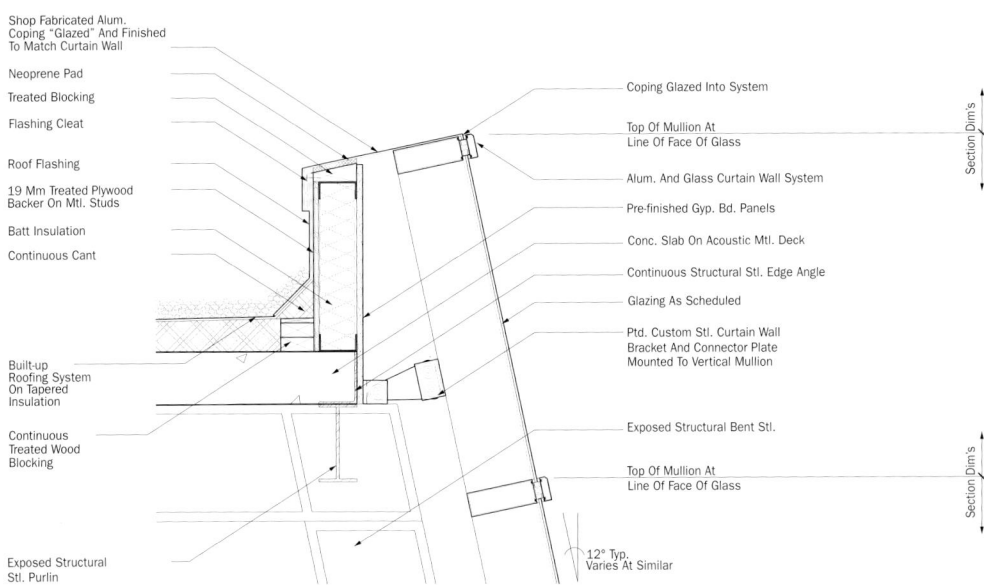
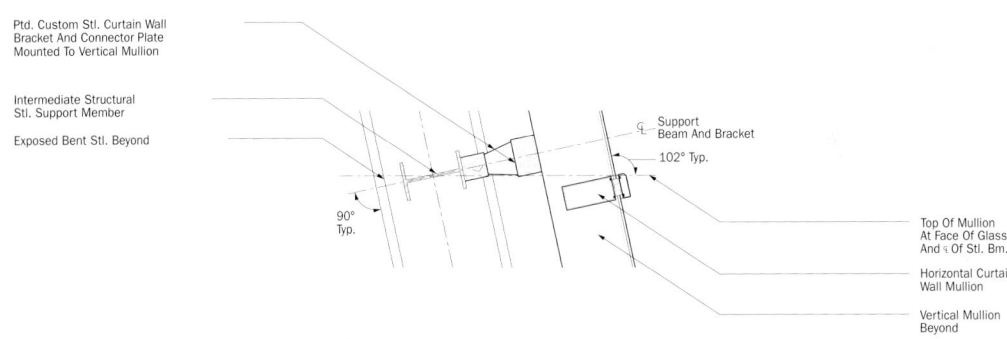
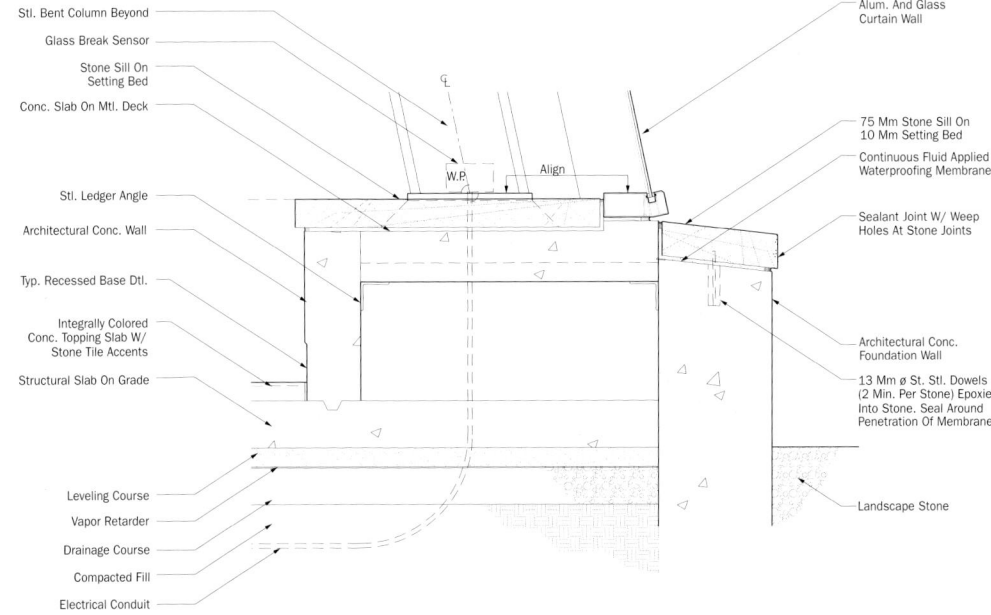

The building's openness and transparency reveal the FDA's intent to use it to build a new, integrated culture of work. Staff members formerly housed in separate testing laboratories and field offices scattered across the city are brought together in one location, sitting side by side in common office neighborhoods in order to foster teamwork. The environment thus promotes a spirit of accessibility and sharing that mirrors the literal transparency offered by glass walls between offices and laboratories. From the beginning of the programming and planning process with the FDA, it was intended that the building would influence explicitly the way the institution functions, to encourage innovation and change in the workplace. Through the design process, and with the unwavering support and participation of the client, the functional program was translated into a dynamic and forward-looking architectural image symbolizing this intent. Overall, the building's remarkable lucidity and spatial fluidity distinguish it.

Laboratories look into offices through full-height walls of glass, and toward the two-story public circulation space beyond. Both abundant natural light and the vista of the wetlands are brought deeply through the open-plan offices into the labs.

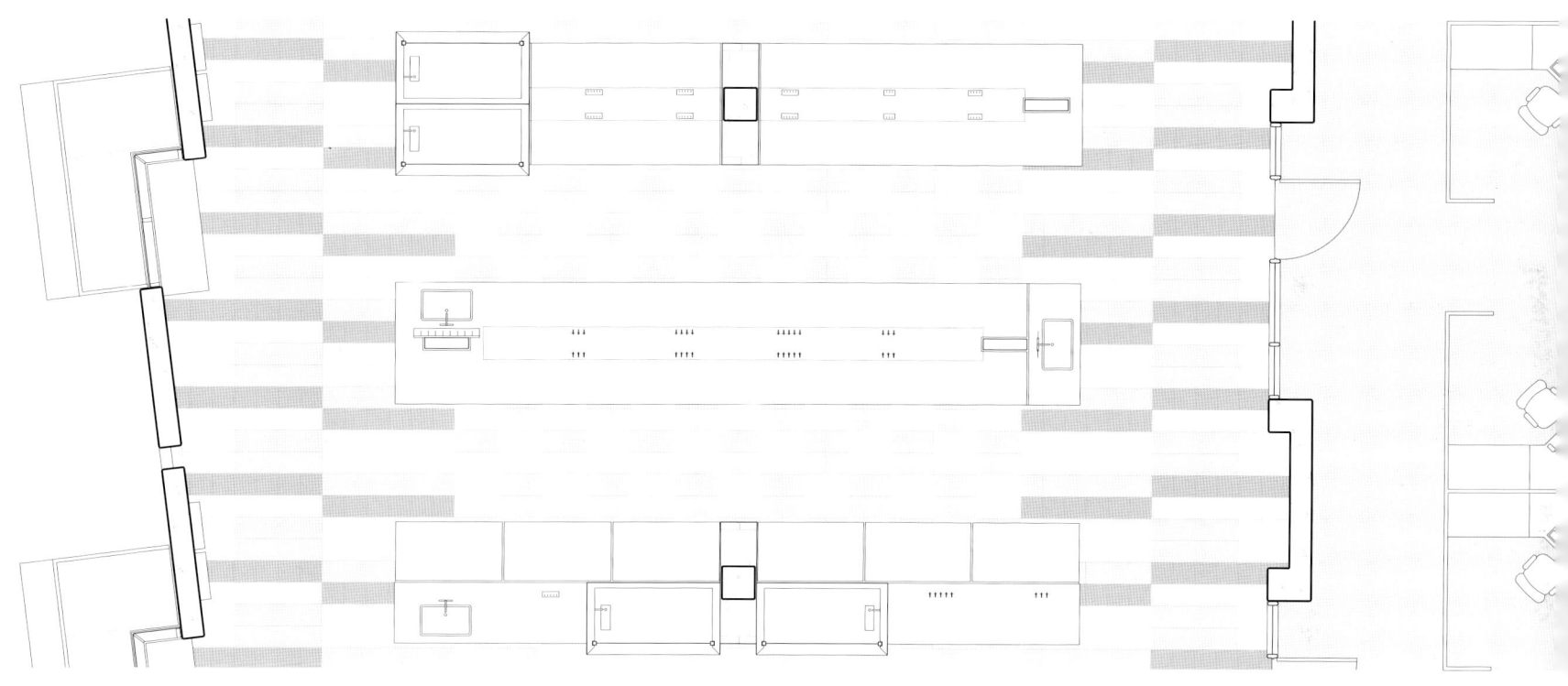

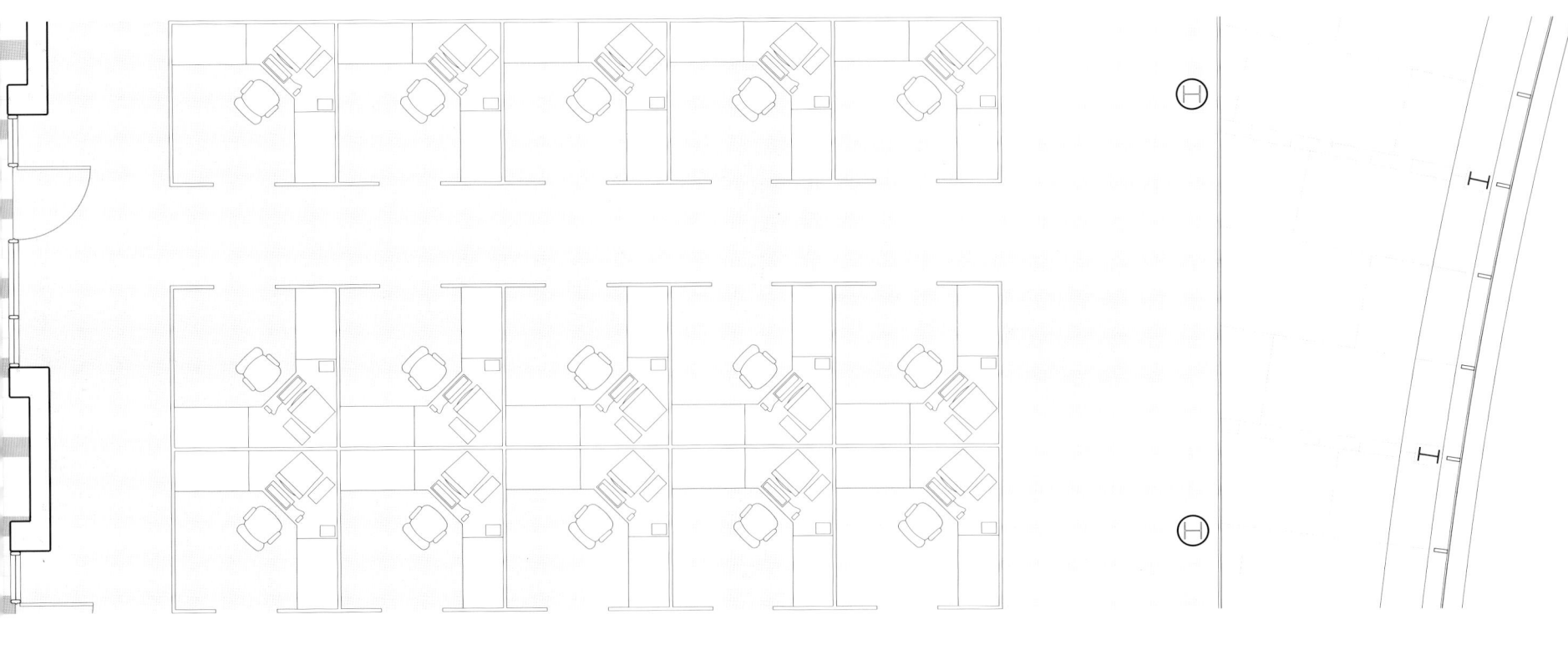

While they are separated environmentally from each other, the laboratories are reached from the offices directly through glass doors. The same lighting fixtures are used in both, but spaced more closely in the labs to achieve the higher light levels desired by the users.

Enclosed private offices borrow natural light through the large open-plan offices, reversing the usual hierarchy where management offices are placed along the exterior wall.

A pair of internal staff circulation aisles is placed between offices and laboratories. Office ceilings are held back to expose the intersections of the steel structure with concrete shear piers which are left in their natural state. Daylight enters this space through a clerestory window above.

Shown on the previous pages, the internal staff aisle in the laboratories is wide enough to accommodate equipment alcoves and is demarcated by its graphic floor pattern.

Angled shear walls of exposed concrete define a series of triangular niches along the outer edge of the laboratory service corridors. These niches are furnished with writing surfaces that support quick clerical tasks associated with lab work. All building support systems are arranged neatly above the corridor space, with floors of the same pronounced graphic pattern. Repetitive modular configuration of systems affords ready access, with the flexibility to shut down and reconfigure any module, without interrupting work in adjacent labs.

In response to its orientation, the building's southwest elevation is a study in the control of solar heat gain, offering a dramatic contrast with the abstract simplicity of the open glass wall facing northeast to the principal views. This façade exudes solidity, as heavy concrete shear walls alternate repetitively with tall bay windows that are protected by four tiers of stainless steel sunscreens to shade the glass. These four horizontal tiers, made necessary by the 17-foot floor-to-floor height of the structure, induce ambiguity in scale. Upon first glance, it is difficult to read the scale of the wall and to know whether the building is only two stories tall, or four. The fact that the three laboratory blocks are expressed clearly and somewhat separately—articulated in between by the broad copper screens sheltering the exterior stairs—only adds to this ambiguity by extending the apparent length of the façade. Unless viewed from some distance, this façade always appears foreshortened. When viewed closely, its horizontal dimensions are read as reduced, in contrast to the vertical emphasis in the glazing and in the detailing of the concrete.

Created by metal frames and perforated surfaces, the play of intricate shadow patterns on the smooth concrete surfaces of the southwest elevation contrasts graphically with the reflective plane of curved glass on the northeast. The former appears rooted to the earth; the latter belongs to the sky above.

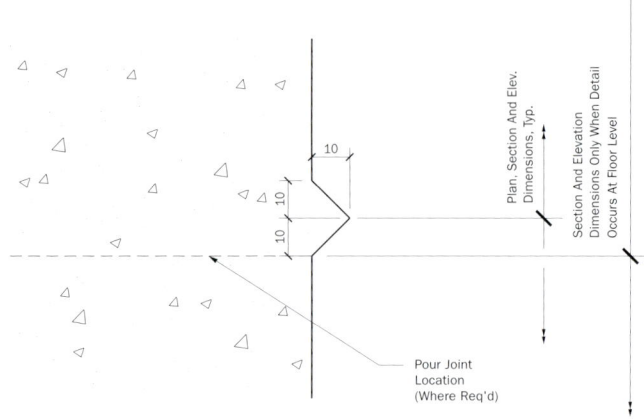

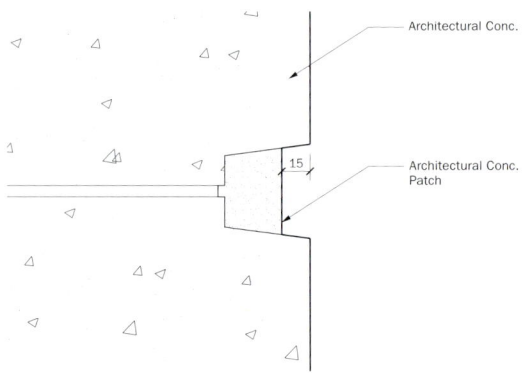

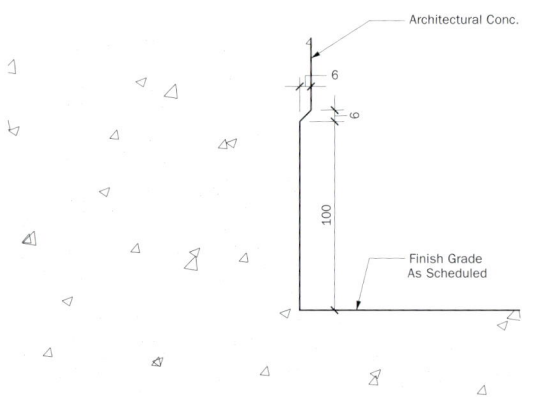

Careful attention to detail brings the concrete walls to life in the soft Southern California light. Vertical formwork was carefully composed of standard sheets of resin-coated plywood with chamfered edges, leaving raised seams that cast shadows on the concrete. Accentuated when light grazes them, these shadow lines can disappear almost entirely at certain times of day. Dotting the wall surface, tie-holes are left exposed and filled only partially with grout.

At regular intervals, glass is set directly into narrow slots carved into the concrete walls, which are detailed precisely to receive the brackets of the sunscreens shading adjacent bay windows.

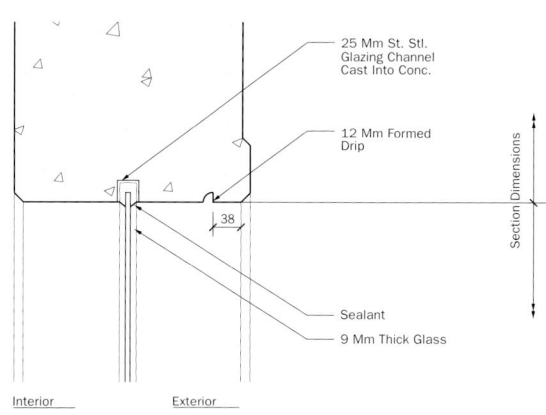
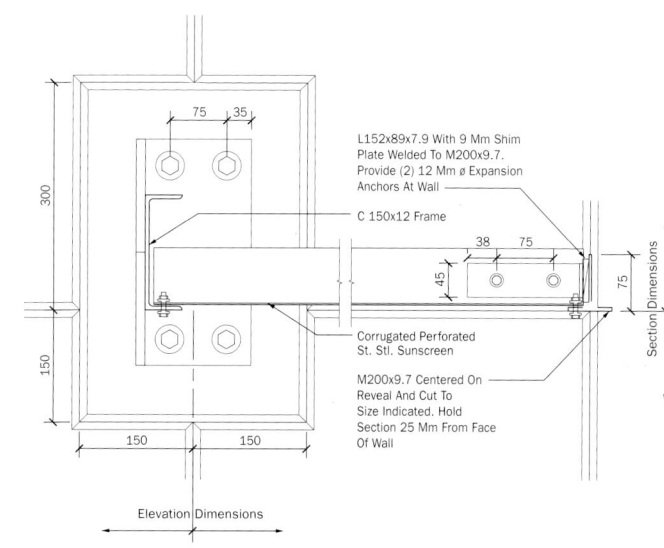
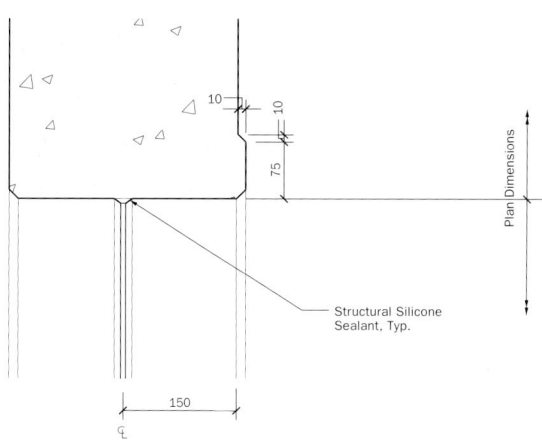
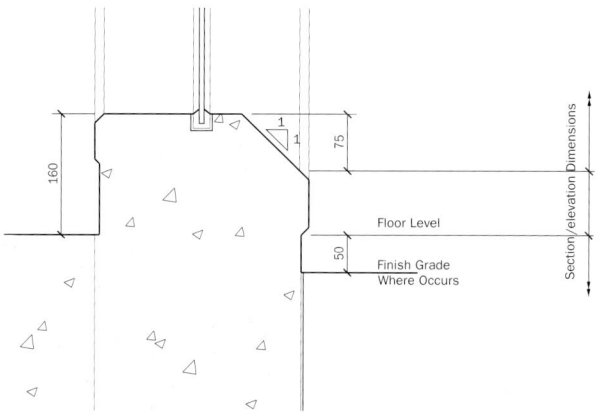

Horizontal sunscreens occur in exuberant profusion on the building's southwest faces. Detailed with painted steel brackets supporting corrugated and perforated sheets of stainless steel, they are quite deep in profile, and are edged by stainless steel "beaks" which reflect the sunlight, especially in the late evening.

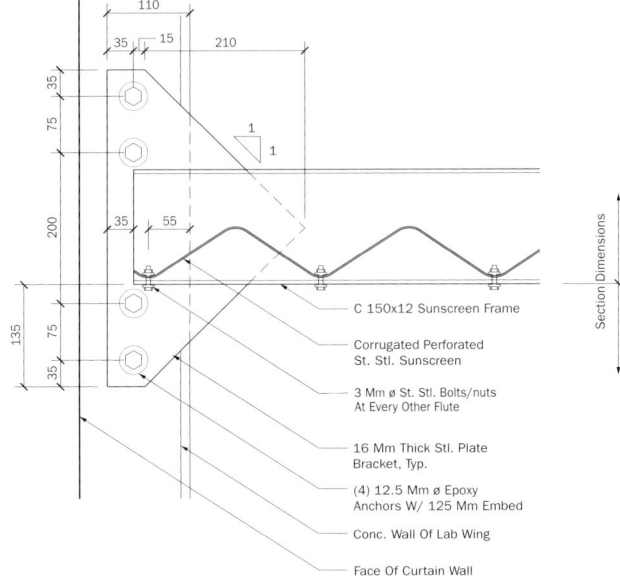

- C 150x12 Sunscreen Frame
- Corrugated Perforated St. Stl. Sunscreen
- 3 Mm ø St. Stl. Bolts/nuts At Every Other Flute
- 16 Mm Thick Stl. Plate Bracket, Typ.
- (4) 12.5 Mm ø Epoxy Anchors W/ 125 Mm Embed
- Conc. Wall Of Lab Wing
- Face Of Curtain Wall

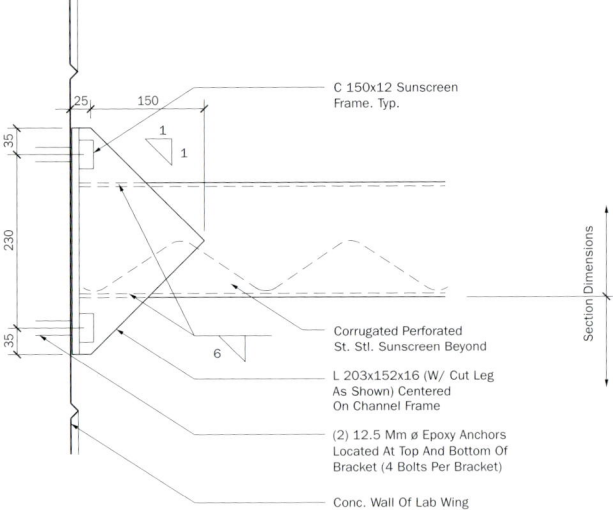

- C 150x12 Sunscreen Frame. Typ.
- Corrugated Perforated St. Stl. Sunscreen Beyond
- L 203x152x16 (W/ Cut Leg As Shown) Centered On Channel Frame
- (2) 12.5 Mm ø Epoxy Anchors Located At Top And Bottom Of Bracket (4 Bolts Per Bracket)
- Conc. Wall Of Lab Wing

Note: Bend Angle To 83° At Bracket And Cut Edge Of Screen To Follow Angle Of Wall Where Adjacent Walls Are Not Parallel

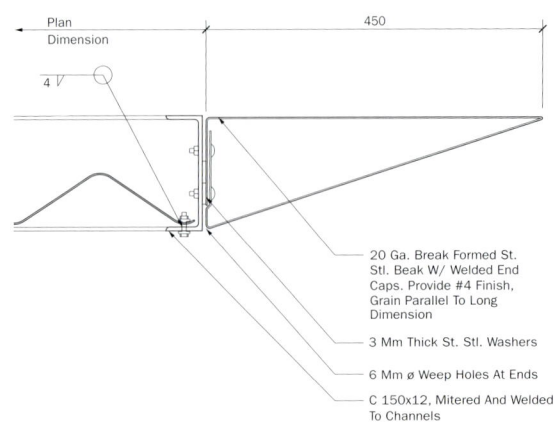

- 20 Ga. Break Formed St. Stl. Beak W/ Welded End Caps. Provide #4 Finish, Grain Parallel To Long Dimension
- 3 Mm Thick St. Stl. Washers
- 6 Mm ø Weep Holes At Ends
- C 150x12, Mitered And Welded To Channels

Four exit stairs flank the three laboratory blocks along the southwest elevation of the building. Although they are not fully enclosed, they are partially surrounded and protected by large copper screen walls. These walls are detailed and assembled in a very straightforward and economical manner. Diaphanous sheets of corrugated and perforated copper are fastened directly to welded tubular steel frames that curve around and are attached to the supporting structures of the stairs. Light is both filtered through the perforations and reflected by the corrugated ridges of the metal surfaces, which appear delicate and translucent in dazzling contrast with the adjacent massive, planar concrete walls. Left unfinished in a natural state, the copper sheets can be expected to age slowly in the Southern California climate, acquiring their usual pale green patina over decades rather than years.

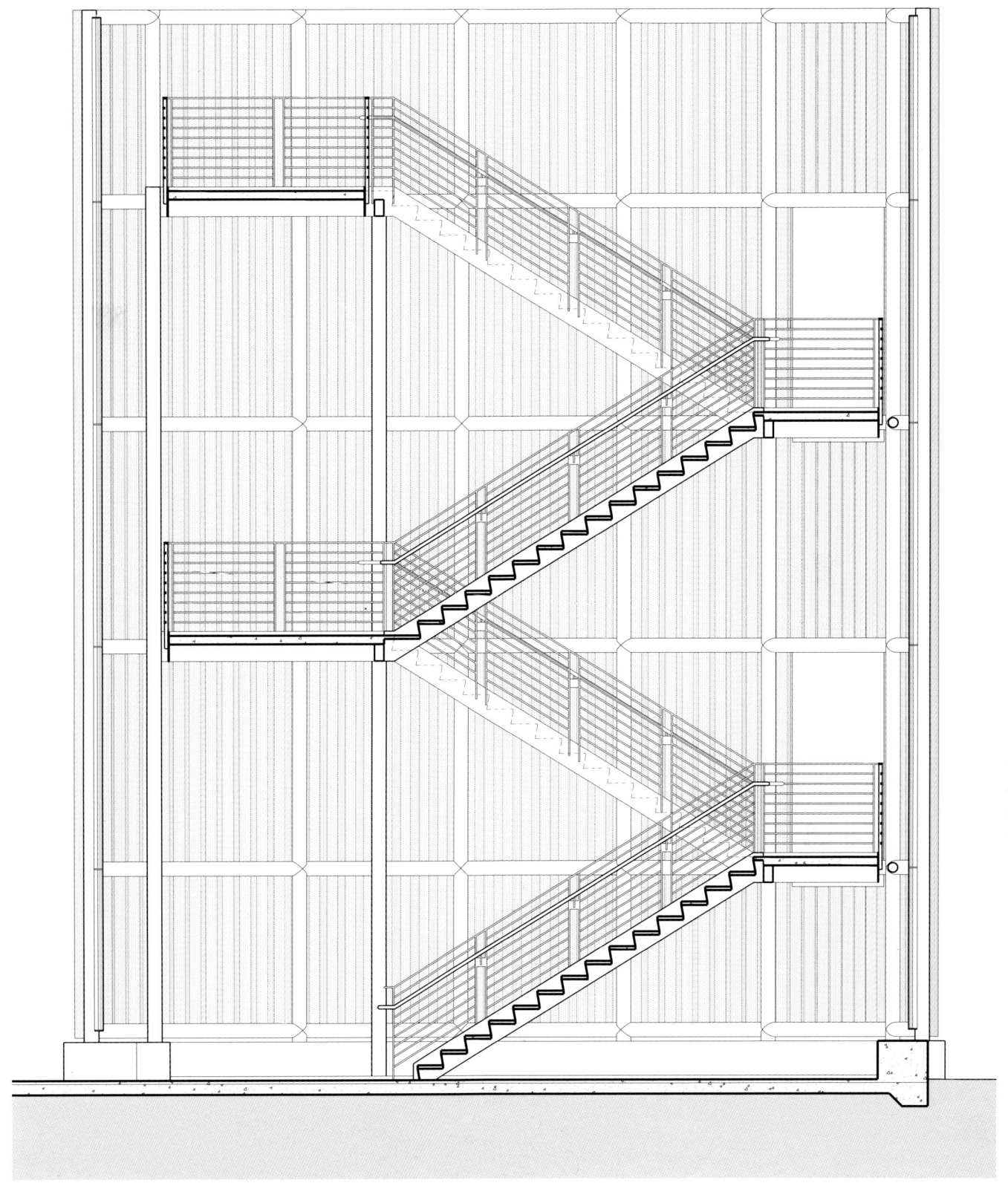

The copper screen walls at the exterior exit stairs are shaped to form protected courtyards, conveniently located within the secure perimeter of the building adjacent to vertical circulation between the two levels of laboratories. Because of their location and the protection they afford from sun and wind, these intimate outdoor spaces are extremely popular with staff members, who use them for breaks and informal meetings.

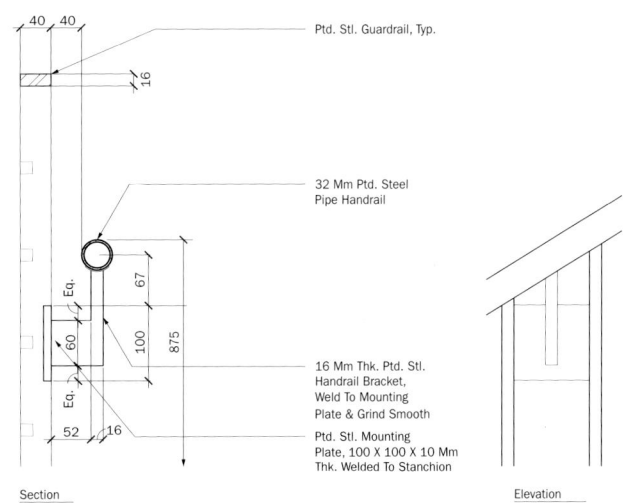
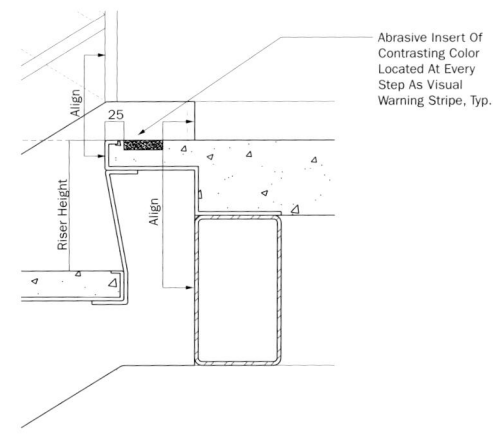
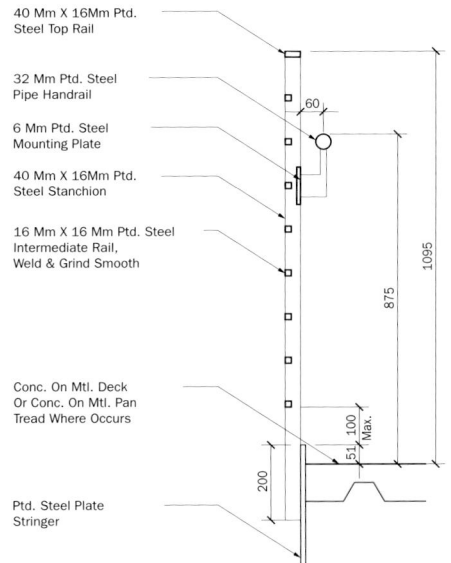
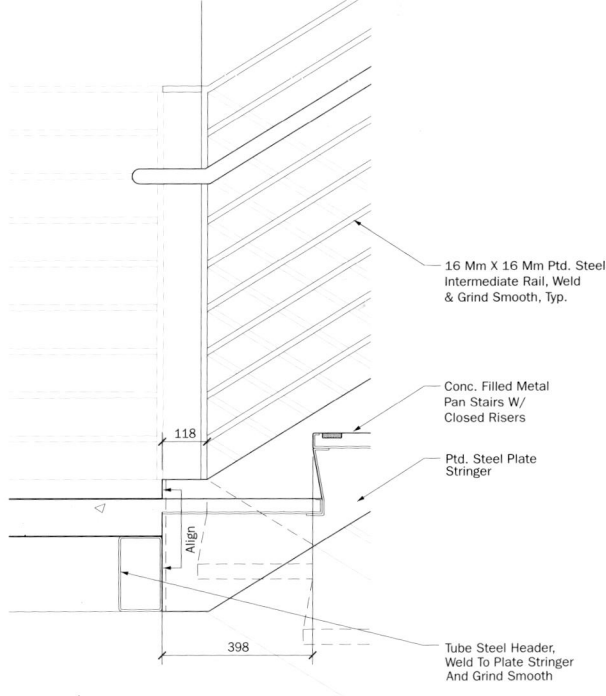

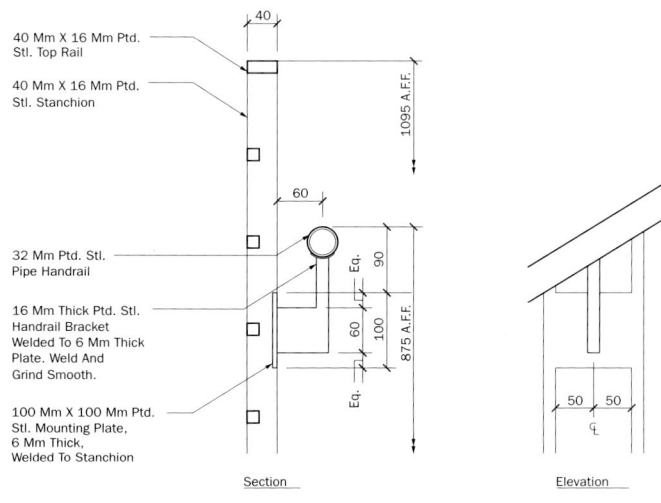
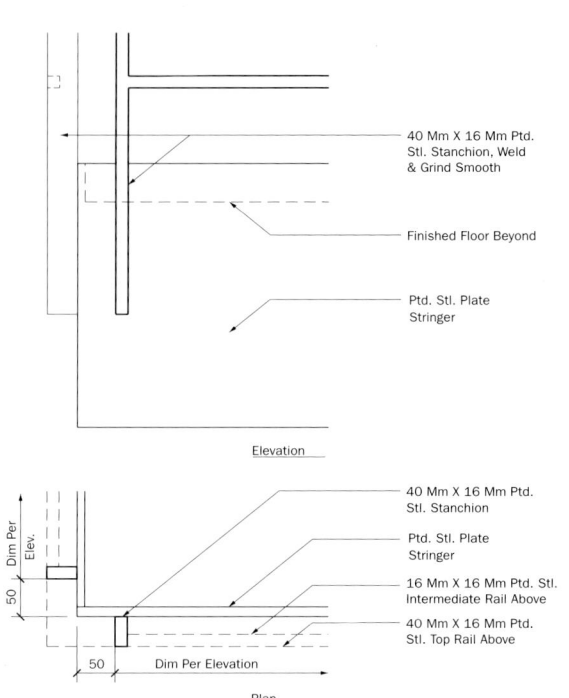
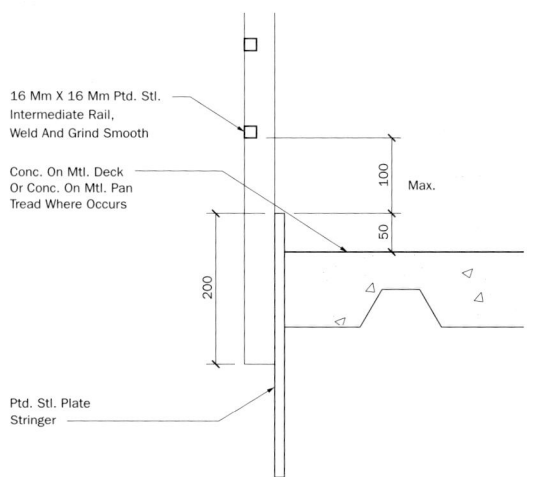
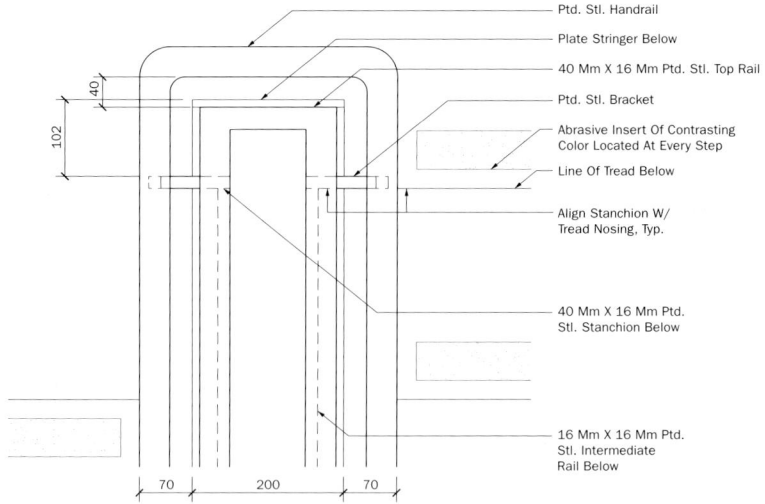

Carefully detailed in the economical spirit of the screen wall structure to which they are attached, the exit stairs are simple steel pans filled with concrete and supported by steel plate stringers. Guard rails are welded and painted steel.

Throughout the day, an intricate play of shadow patterns is projected onto the concrete by the perforated screen walls, exit stairs, and their supporting structures. Intermediate stair landings extend through "windows" cut into the copper screens, framing views of the Upper Newport Bay landscape to the west.

Facing the street and the site's main entry, the relatively narrow end of the building is dominated by the curved copper screen wall of the conference center. This wall thrusts powerfully outward and skirts the ground below, emphatic in its horizontality. To the far left of the composition, the curved glass wall of the northeast elevation ends in a line just as emphatically vertical. The downward sloping curve of glass folds gently over to slope upward at this point, reaching out to enclose a deep void and forming a monumental two-story entrance porch, beckoning from the street. Adjacent to the porch, as the curve folds, the wall's glazing falls away gradually in horizontal layers, opening up the aluminum grid into a trellis with a windscreen at its base. Protected from the elements, this porch represents, on the entrance façade, the position—in section—of the glazed two-story circulation spine that runs the length of the building. In order to reach the spine, however, one first must pass through the low-ceilinged foyer inside the entrance.

At the entrance porch, the curved glass wall terminates in the form of a prow, while the roof above is edged by a wing-shaped stainless steel fin (or "beak") projected on painted steel brackets. The upward curve of this fin is configured to oppose and complement the downward curve of the conference center façade.

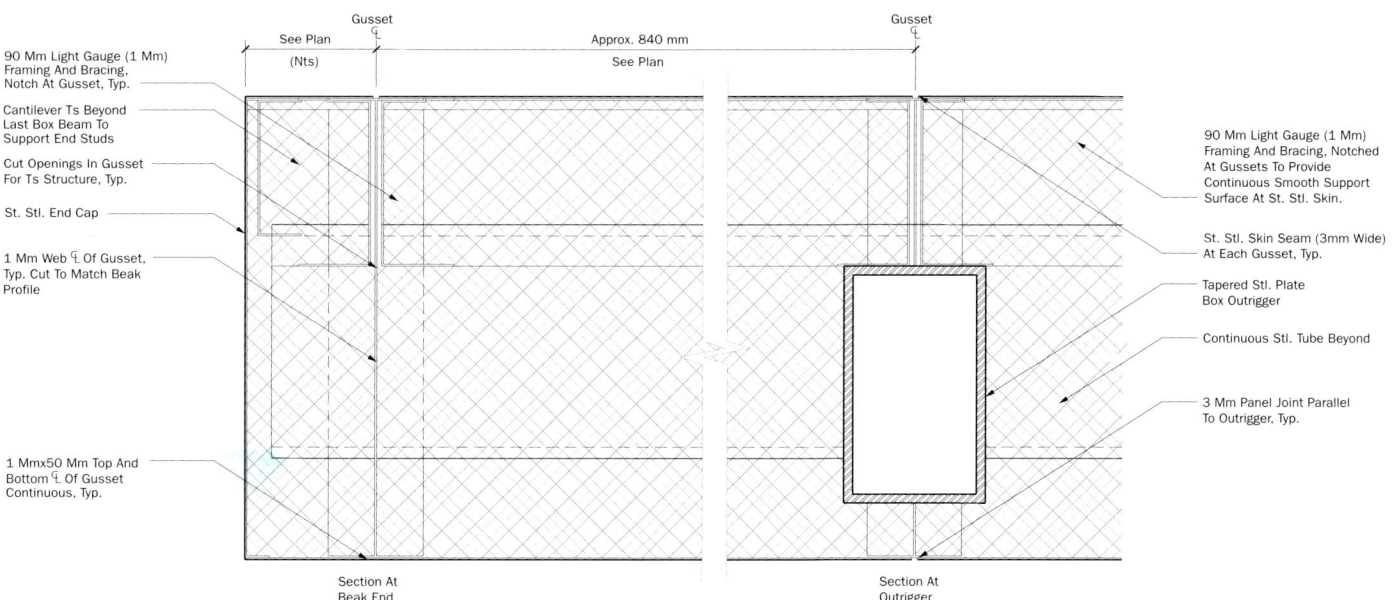
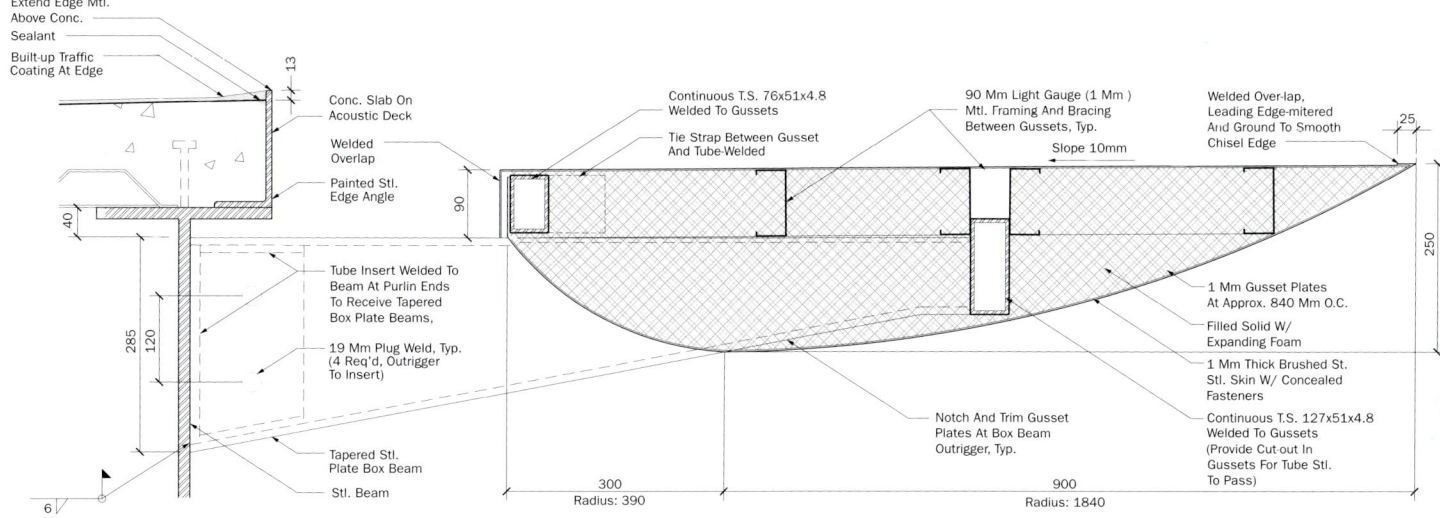

The standing seam copper roof of the conference center changes at the second floor roofline into a perforated copper screen, pulled down over the windows to the directors' offices and meeting rooms below. This screen floats beyond the stepped vertical wall behind it, leaving the glass accessible for cleaning.

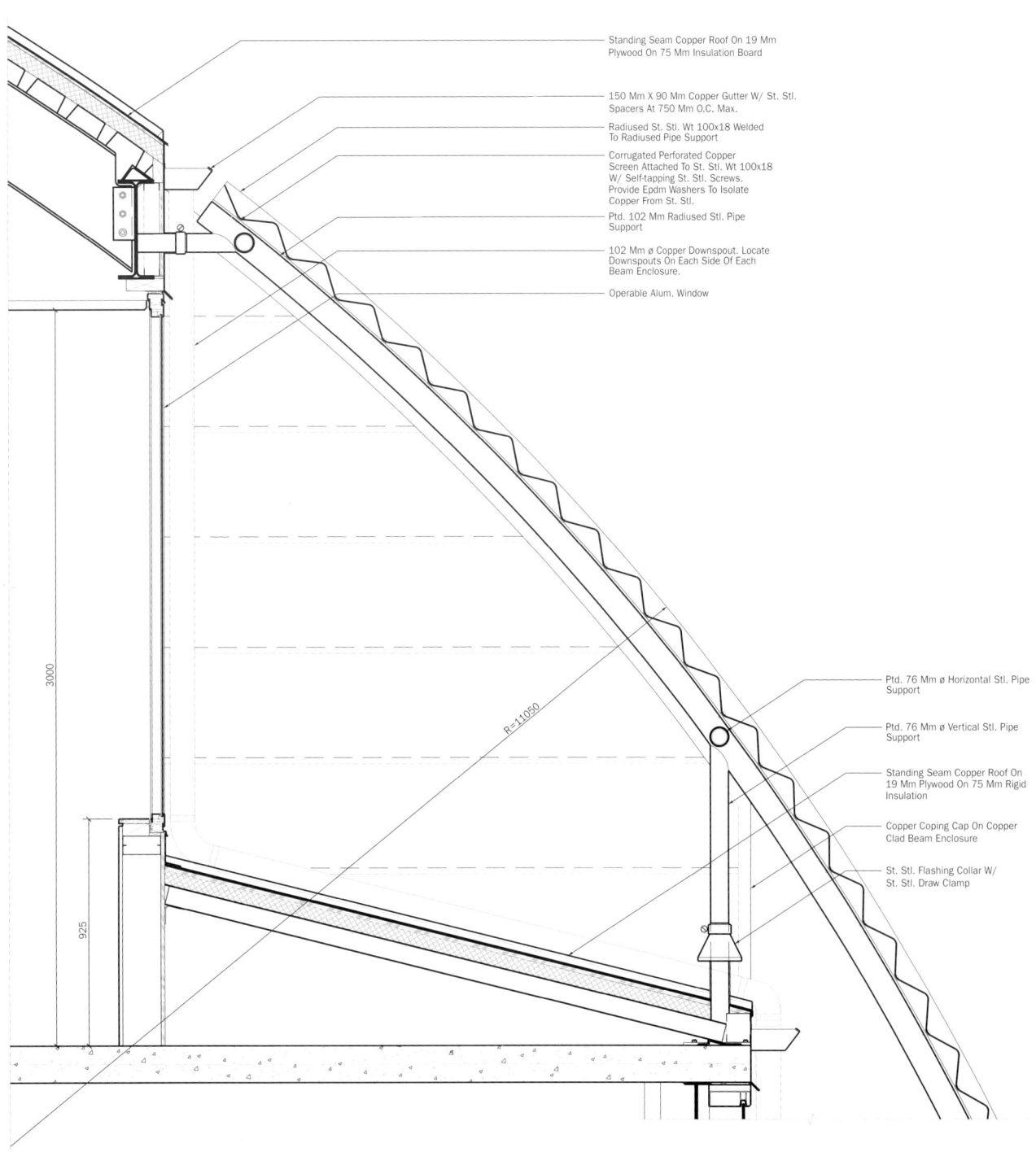

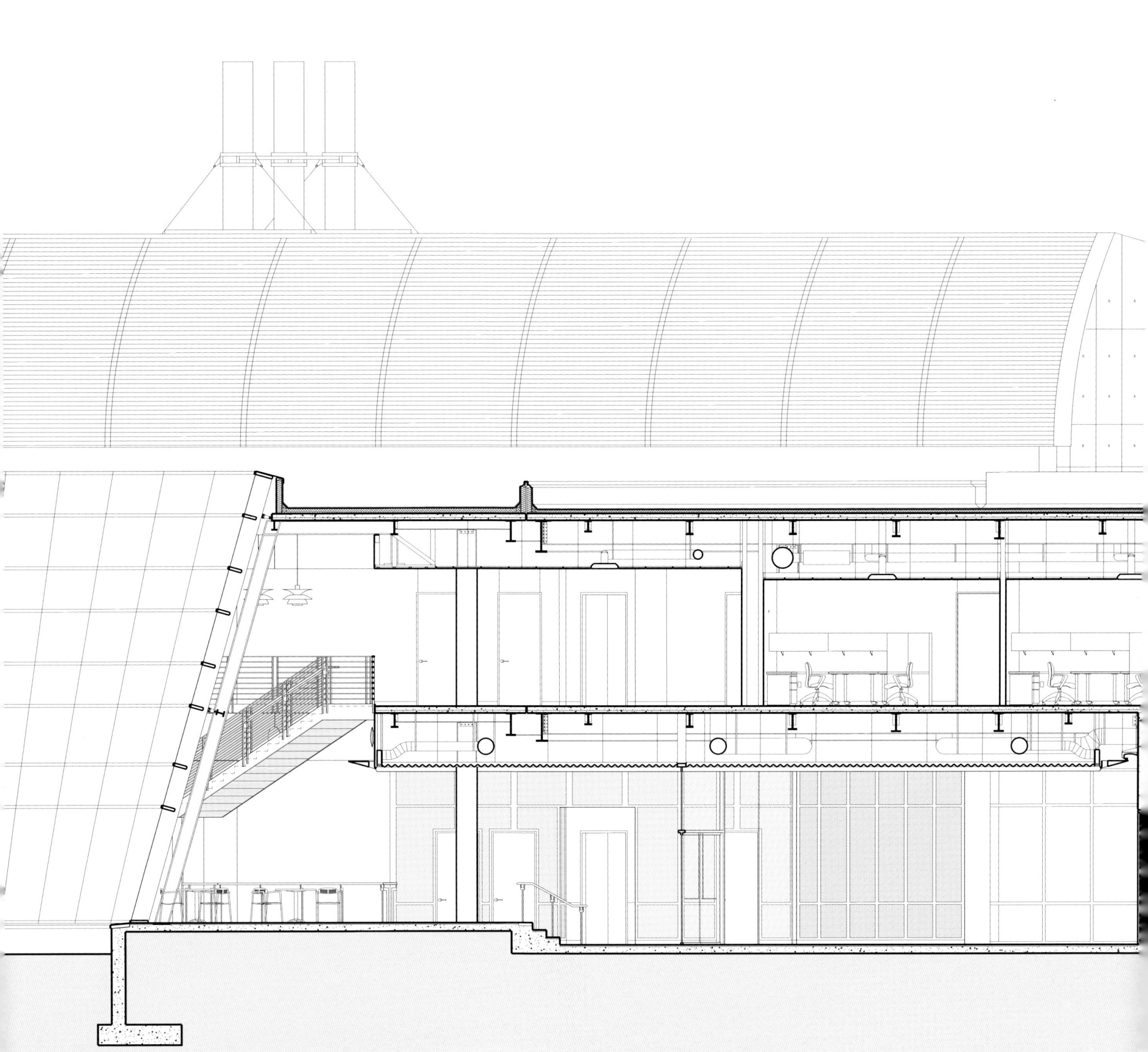

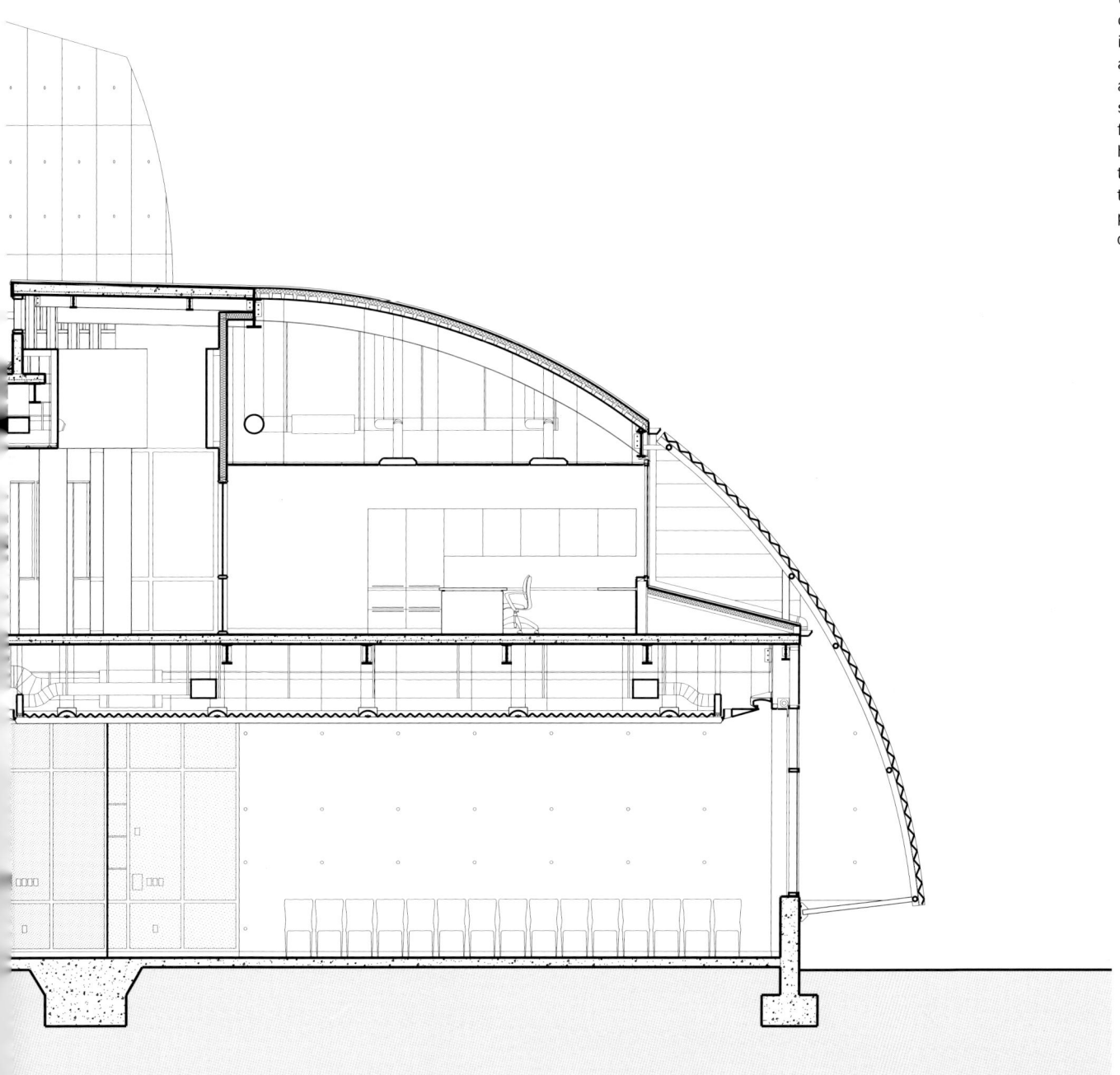

Externally, the conference center mass is expressed as a separate sculptural element; internally, it connects seamlessly on both levels with the balance of the building. Just inside the lower level entrance foyer, a security desk overlooks a generous lobby, which also functions as a breakout space for the conference center. The large meeting room, as well as the lobby and adjacent courtyard, is located outside the secure perimeter of laboratories and offices, so that they can be used by visitors from the outside community as well as by staff, with no interruption or compromise to the everyday activities of the FDA. Tucked into the second level above the conference center, behind the curved screen wall, is a suite of five private offices for departmental directors, as well as spaces to house their administrative staff. Along with the regional director's office, located adjacent to them, these building areas require the most public access, which dictated their placement close to the main entrance.

A framework of welded steel tubes supports curved stainless steel ribs, to which the corrugated copper panels of the screen are attached directly. To prevent intrusion of rainwater, stainless steel plates finish the top edges of the adjacent concrete walls.

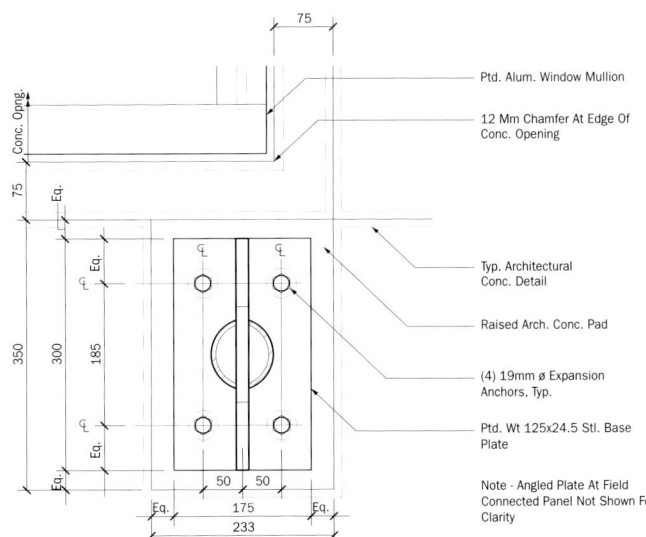
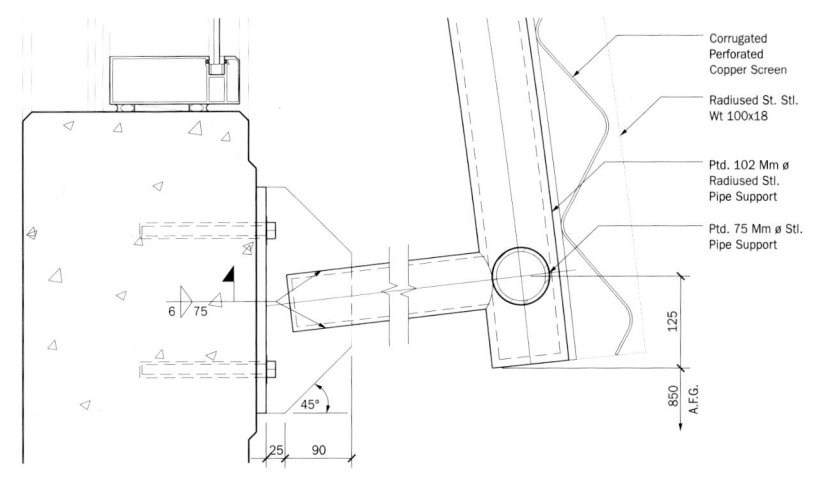
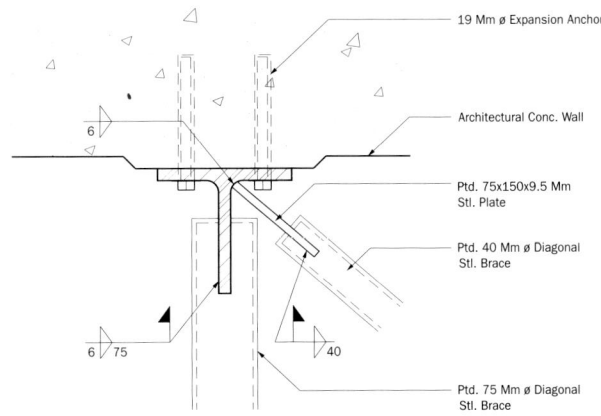
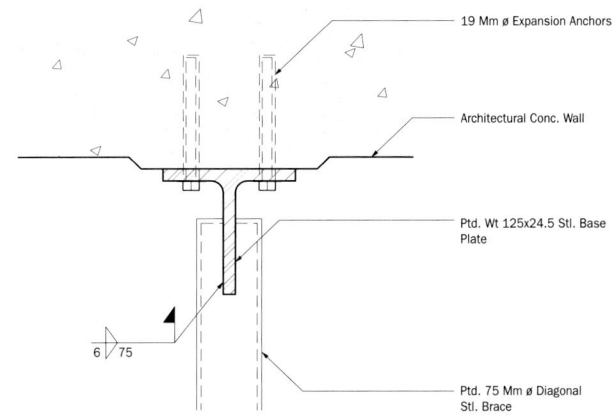
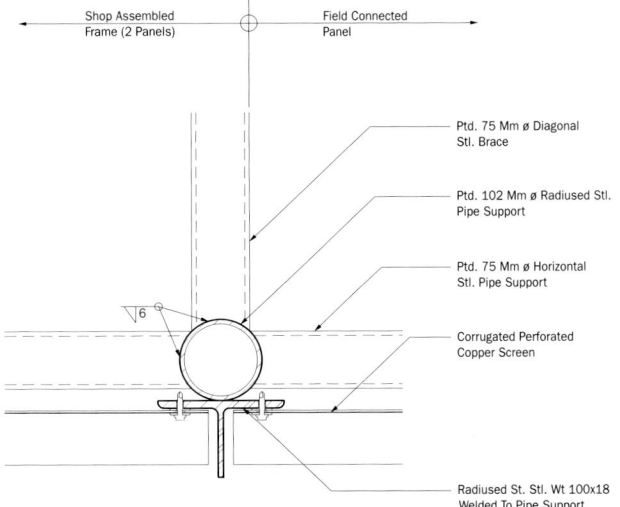
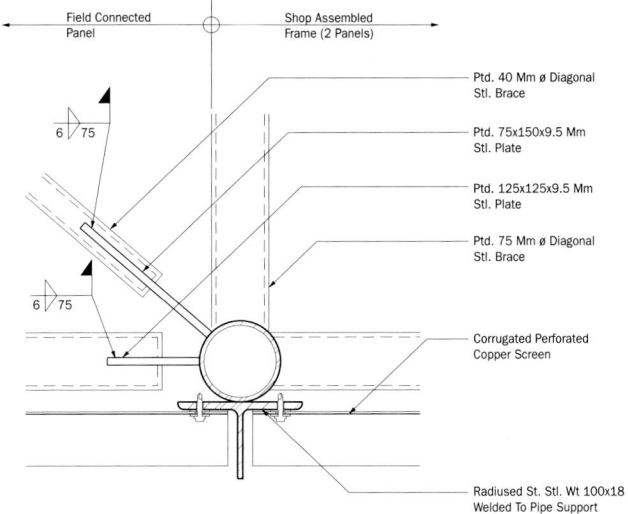

Tapered wooden ribs are employed in the lobby to frame ceiling panels of the same corrugated and perforated stainless steel used in the external sunscreens. They are backed with acoustical material. This ceiling continues beyond the glass security wall that separates public from staff spaces, increasing the apparent size of the lobby.

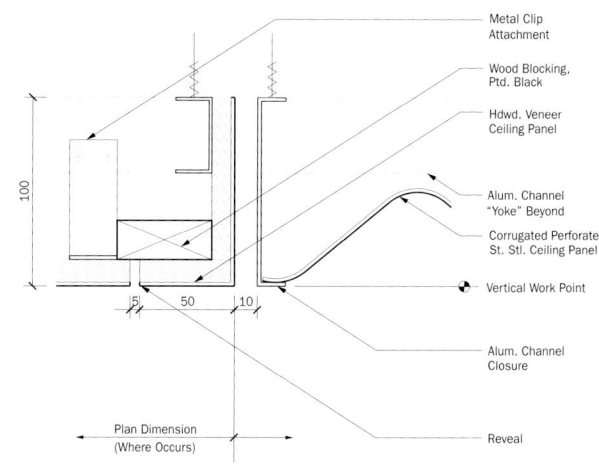

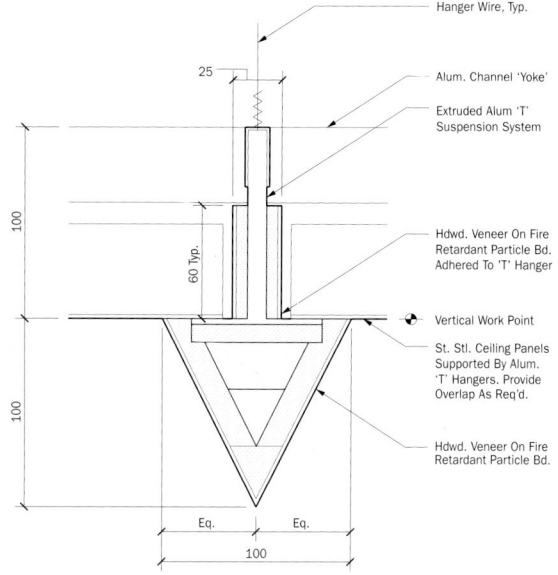

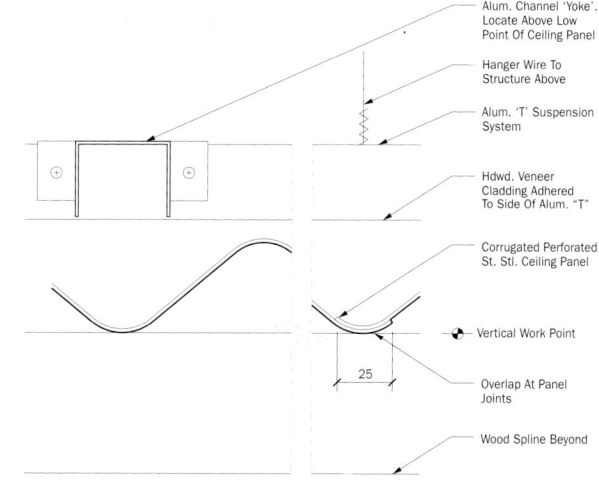

Through the lobby, the view opens into one of the intimate courtyards flanking the laboratory blocks. It is reached through glass doors and extends the social space serving the conference center located on the right.

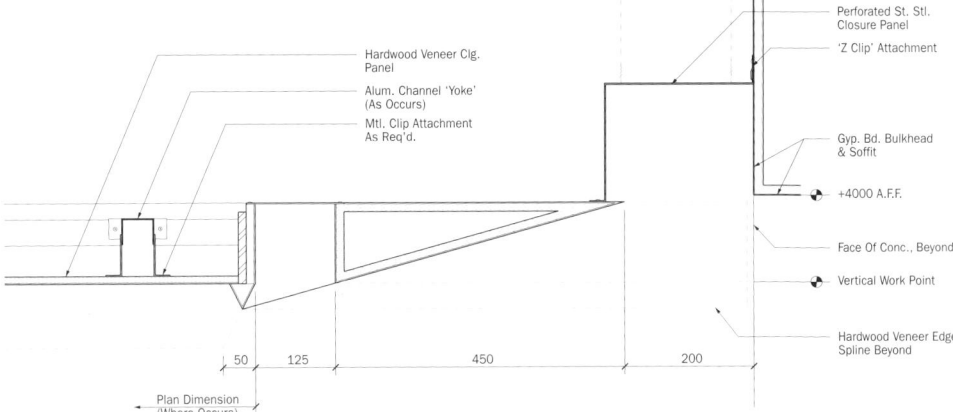

Poured-in-place concrete walls are expressed on the interior of the conference room, which can be subdivided into three smaller spaces. Indirect lighting fixtures are set flush with corrugated ceiling panels matching those in the lobby.

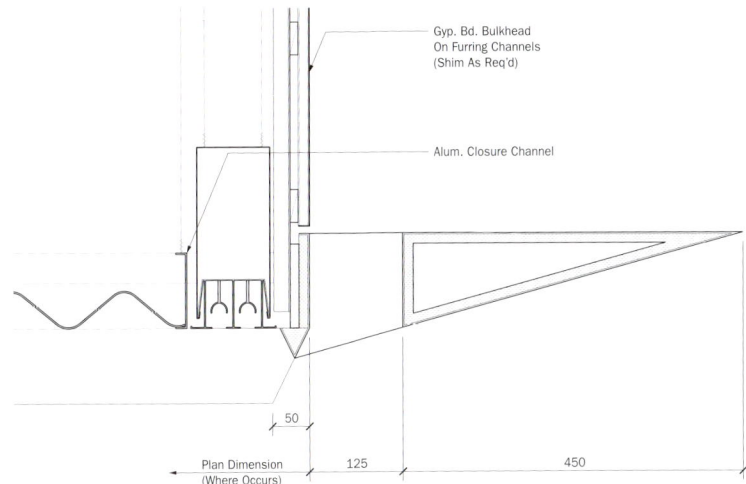

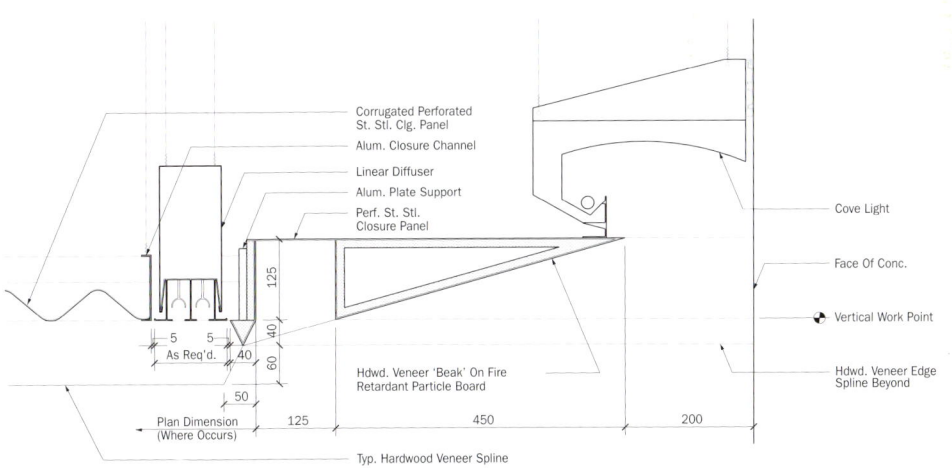

On the second level, the corridor leading to the directors' offices receives daylight from the far end as well as from a clerestory above. Front walls of the offices on the right are glazed to admit natural light into administrative support offices across the corridor.

The curved copper sunscreen, through which neighboring buildings can be seen, protects the directors' offices from the harsh west light and accompanying heat gain. These offices are generous enough in size to accommodate small meetings with staff and visitors.

At the building's main entry, the back wall of the entry porch belongs to a delicately detailed pavilion within the curved glass wall of the northeast elevation. The lower level of this pavilion houses a staff break area with covered outdoor dining terraces overlooking the wetlands. This break area also can be reached from the main lobby, outside the secure perimeter, so that vending machines are accessible to visitors to the conference center. Above, on the second level, is the regional director's office with its contiguous conference room. Both open onto balconies which command sweeping views of the wetlands and mountains. The sloped glass wall, continuous above the cast-in-place concrete "eyebrow" sheltering these balconies, forms a clerestory admitting natural light to the office and conference room.

OVERLEAF: Detailing of steel supporting structure and perforated metal deck also continues from the adjacent two-story circulation spine into these spaces.

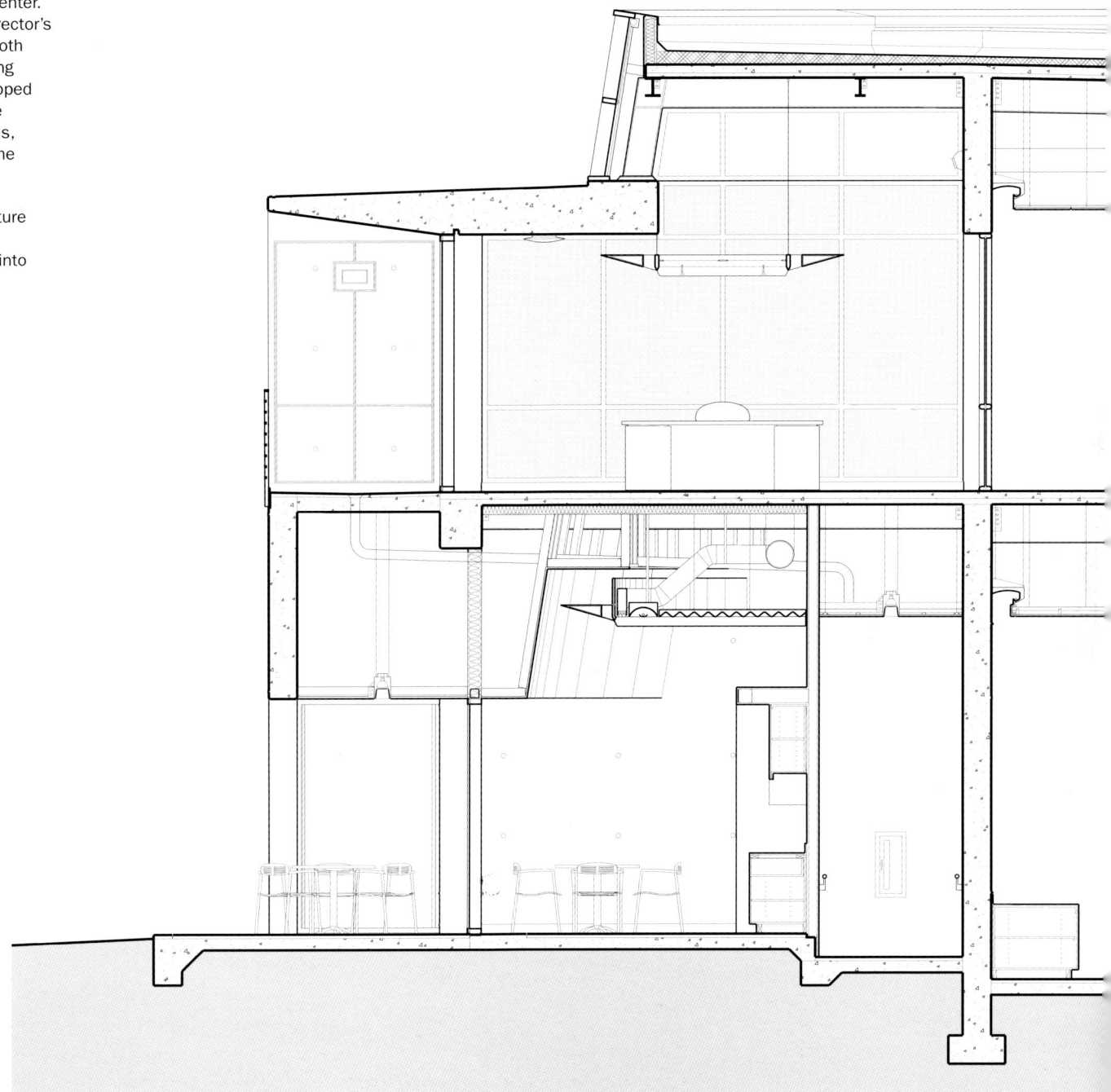

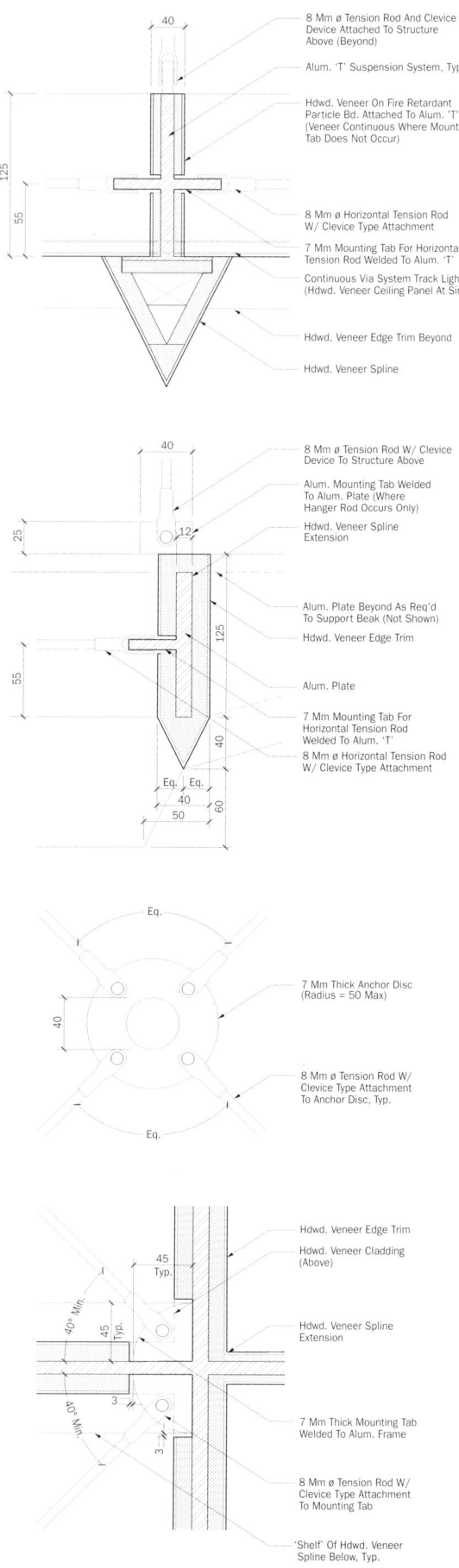

Concrete exterior walls and the "eyebrow" above are exposed on the interior of the director's office and conference room, and both are enriched through the use of wood paneling. A suspended wooden frame (or "chandelier") hovers within to light these spaces, which are separated by glass at the level of the clerestory.

The two-story circulation spine widens at three points along its length, opening up to accommodate free-standing stairs. Colonnades of concrete-encased steel columns line the front of open-plan offices overlooking this space, which is lighted and ventilated from the stepped fascia between the first and second levels. The floor is paved with integrally colored concrete, accented by stripes of polished German limestone. The same stone is employed both outside as a sill and inside as a cap for the seat wall at the base of the sloped glass wall. Likewise it is used as a coping on flanking walls and at the raised seating platforms beneath the stairs. The stairs appear as floating elements in the space, and are supported at their intermediate landings by painted steel columns, in order to keep the superstructure as light as possible in appearance.

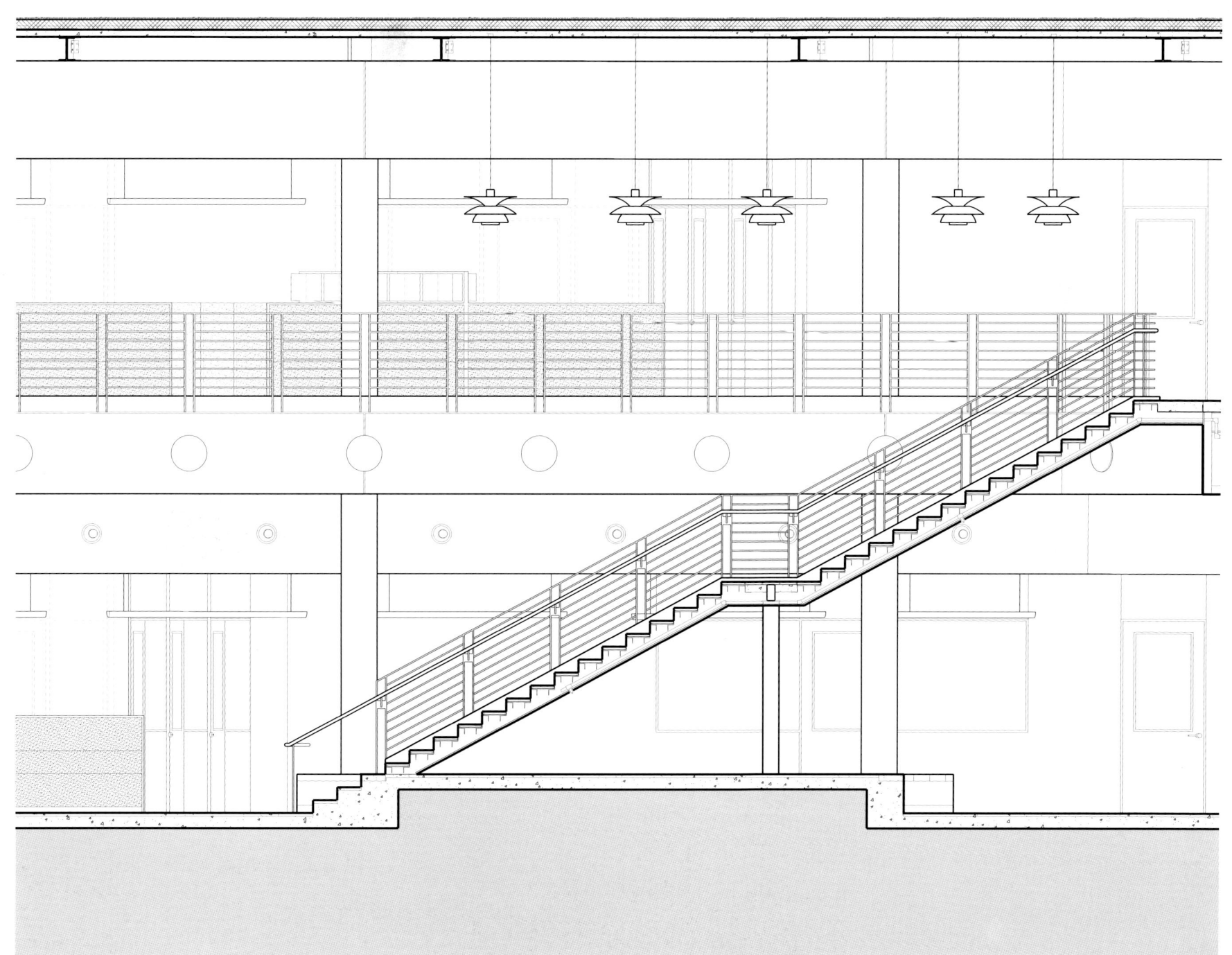

Interior stairs are detailed with the same painted steel-plate stringers and guardrails as the exterior exit stairs. Treads are polished German limestone and handrails are wood. Risers are stainless steel, and perforated stainless steel panels line the stair soffits.

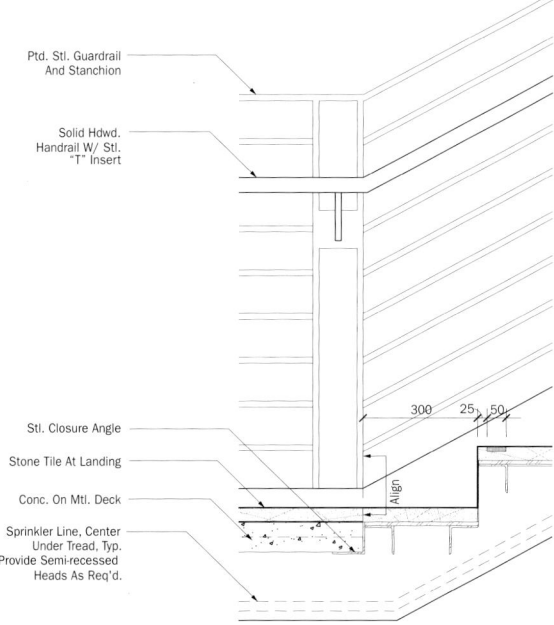
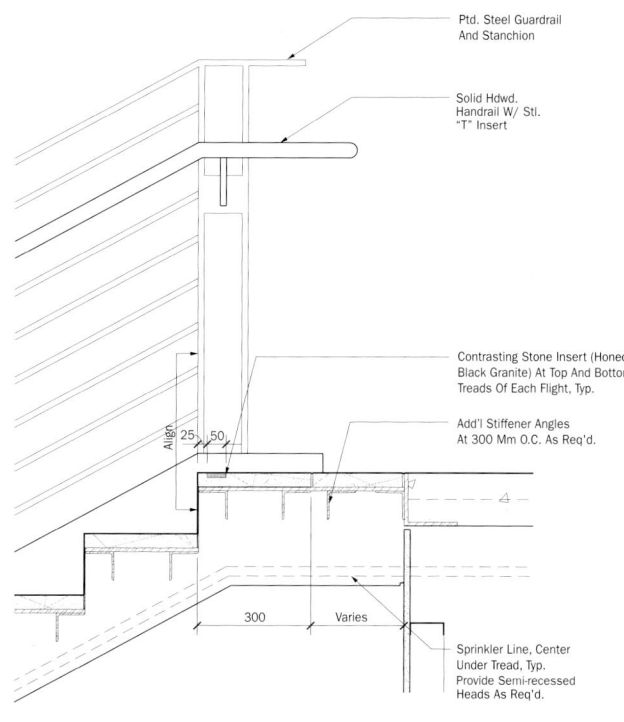
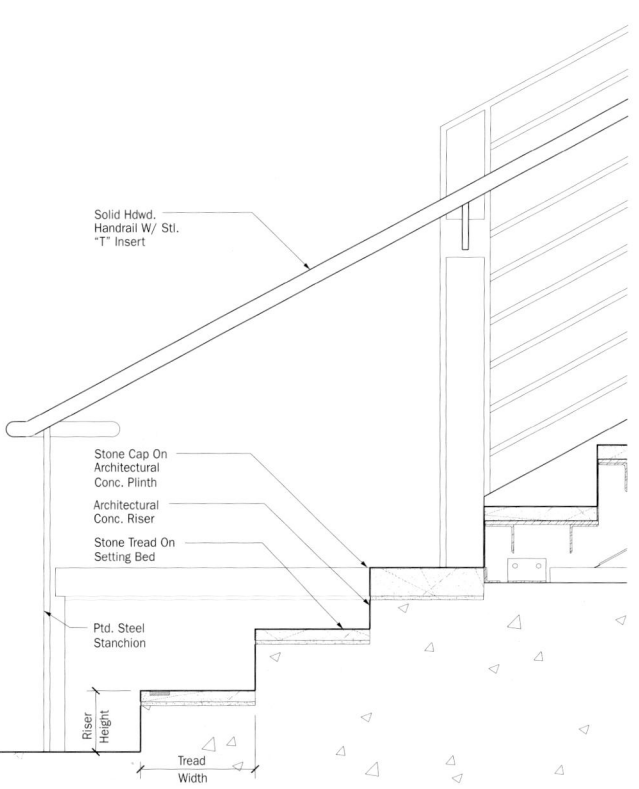
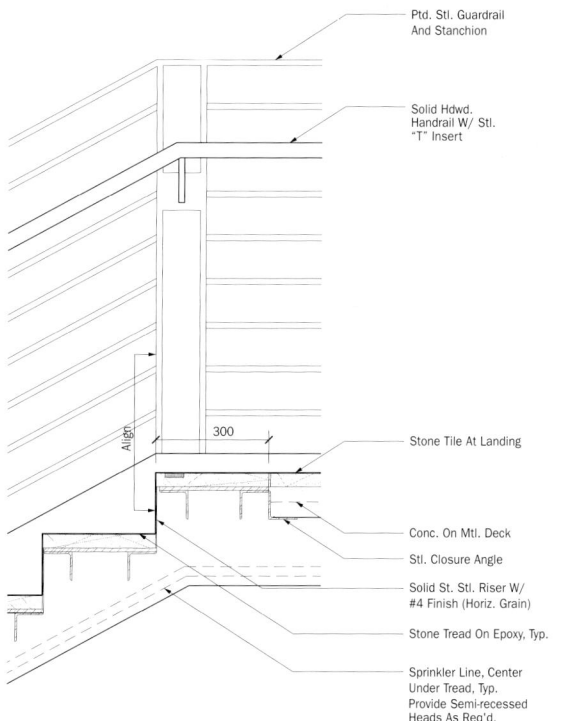

Fritted glass modulates light and decreases sky glare in the two-story spine. Open nodes of meeting and interaction space occur at the stairs; each works like a small piazza overlooking the constant activity of the interior street.

In contrast to the active spaces facing the street, other gathering places in the building are sequestered and intimate in scale.

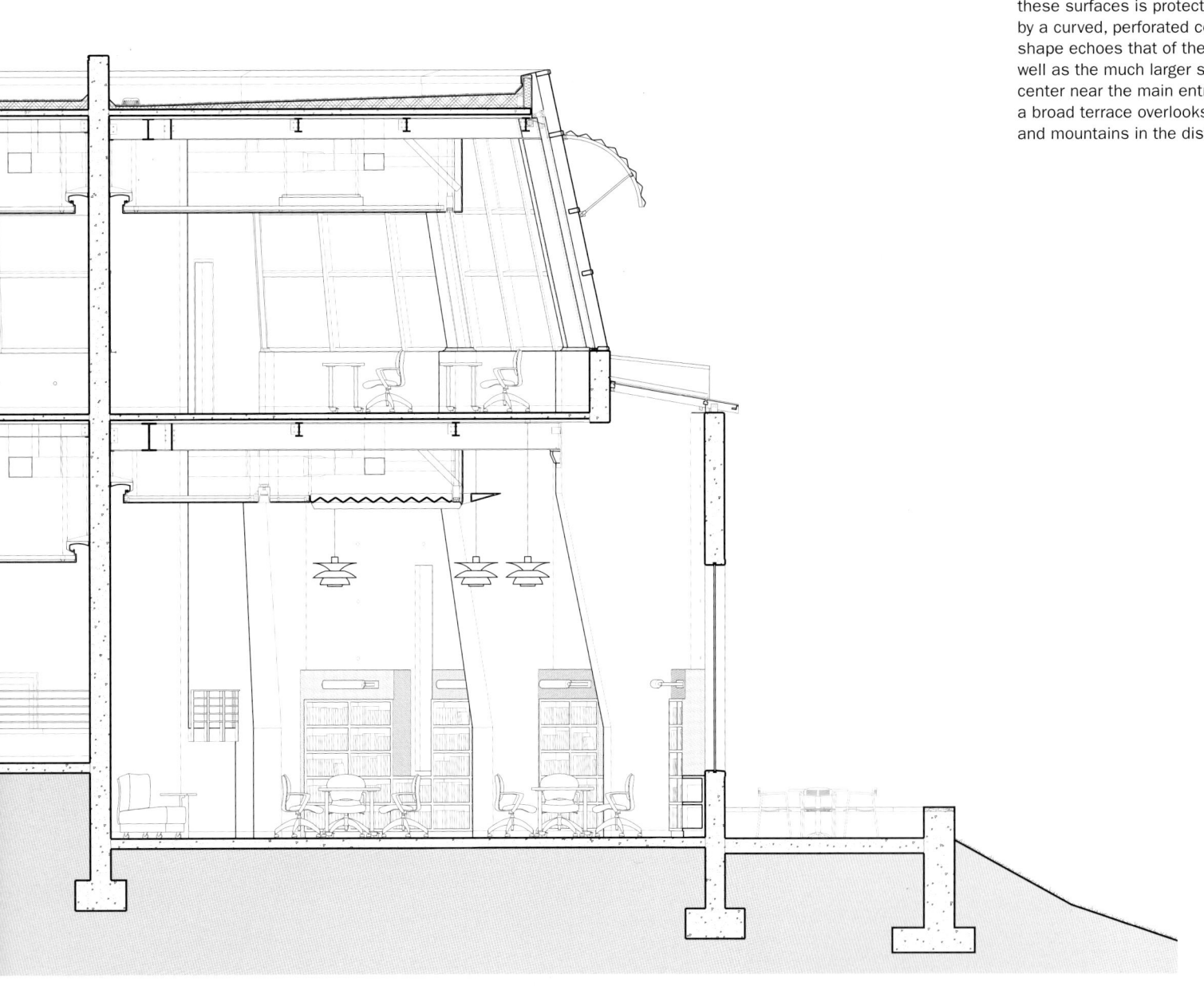

The sloped glass wall on the building's northeast elevation is terminated on its southeast flank by a tower-like form housing the library. A semicircular wall of cast-in-place concrete is detailed with the same raised pattern of seams that occurs on the walls of the laboratory blocks. Likewise this wall is punctuated by narrow glazed slots. On the second level, the semicircle of the training room is set back to allow light to wash down into the library's interior through fritted glass skylights. The mass of the library below interlocks with the long sweep of the glass wall, while the glass is carried through above, as a series of planar facets enclosing the upper level training room. Each of these surfaces is protected from the southern sun by a curved, perforated copper sunscreen whose shape echoes that of the penthouse screens, as well as the much larger screen over the conference center near the main entrance. At the library level, a broad terrace overlooks the wetland sanctuary and mountains in the distance.

Within the semicircular library space, a series of concrete piers are positioned to support the floor above, while allowing natural light to enter from the perimeter. The piers break down the tall space into alcoves lined with pale wooden bookcases. Above is a fan-shaped version of the wood and stainless steel ceiling in the main lobby and conference center. The resulting space, open only through the narrow slots to the exterior, is subdued and monastic in quality—exuding a spirit quite different from the openness and transparency elsewhere in the building.

Natural light suffuses the outer concrete walls and piers of the library at all times of day, in all seasons of the year. The linear frit pattern of the sloped glass skylights is rendered as a pattern of soft arcs on the curved wall surface below.

As the public circulation route terminates, the library is situated a half-level below the first floor of the main building, which overlooks it, taking advantage of the site's slope. As a result, the library—reached via a gentle ramp—enjoys a degree of separation and seclusion from activities in the offices and laboratories.

If the library is the structure's most cloistered space, the training room above it is the most open. It is surrounded on all sides with glass, offering the widest panoramic views anywhere in the building. Outside the glass wall, copper sunscreens are attached directly to curved stainless steel bents supported by tubular struts. The room can be darkened by lowering fabric shades at its perimeter.

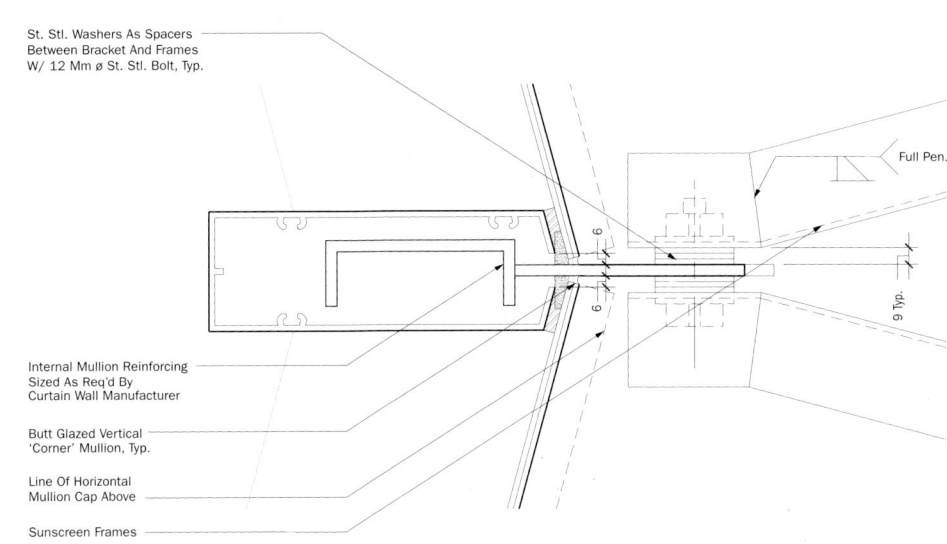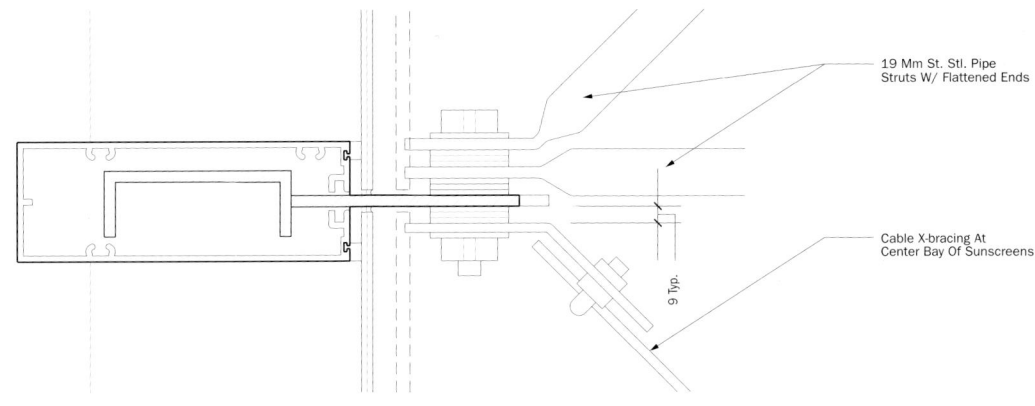

Seen from the wetlands below, the concrete walls of the terrace and of the library above plant the end of the building firmly into its sloping site.

Acknowledgments

I want to thank our supportive client, consultant, and contractor team members, past and present, for their individual and collective contributions to producing FDA at Irvine. A project that spans eight years of planning, design, funding, and construction requires the talent and extraordinary dedication of a multitude of contributors along the way. Although the entire group includes far too many to list here, I would like to recognize a few individuals without whose commitment this building would not have approached its full potential.

When the FDA announced plans to consolidate the 50-year-old Los Angeles Laboratory and District Office in Irvine, they wanted a facility that would match their changing culture, image, and new work methods. RADM Brenda Holman, Regional Director, along with Doug Hamilton, Office of Management/Center for Drug Evaluation and Research; Alonza Cruse, District Director; and John Wiskerchen, former Seattle Director, envisioned the kind of environment that would both foster increased teamwork and support advances in science and technology. It is their initiative that truly set the project into motion. Patricia Calhoun, Contracting Officer, and Clyde Messerly, Chief, Engineering & Construction Branch, were the stewards of the process, working with the team to ensure that the building not only fulfilled its program needs but maintained the integrity of the design intent, and made it a pleasure to attend job meetings. Day-by-day, Julie Henderson, Facility Manager, tackled the myriad issues that arose, and, with great diplomacy, made it all happen. Our colleagues from HDR, led by Randy Niehaus, and Brian Brown of Hensel Phelps, are truly builders and were our partners throughout the implementation. From our own firm, I would like to recognize my partner, Ted Hyman, for providing the executive leadership essential for guiding the team through the design and construction process, and Dusty Rhoads, my partner in design, for his collaboration in addressing every aspect of the program and architecture—from its sensitive siting to the crafting of the smallest of building details. Equally important were the efforts of James Woolum and Debbie Munson, who worked to bring quality to the interiors consistent with our intentions for the building. Stuart Baur, our project architect—an intern when we were awarded the building and an associate when we finished—ultimately owned every aspect of the design, and his passion for quality and consistency was reflected in the eyes of every subcontractor in the field. And, finally, I would like to acknowledge Deb Barbour, Stacey Williams, and Nancy Fishman, for providing the energy that propelled this monograph to completion. It is with great pride that I thank them all for the quality of their effort.

Doss Mabe

Credits

FDA at Irvine
Irvine, California

Owner
US Food & Drug Administration:
Alonza Cruse, Julie Henderson, Elizabeth Keville, William Hoffman, Ernie Lunsford, Clyde Messerly, Patricia Calhoun

Architects | Engineers
Zimmer Gunsul Frasca Partnership/
Henningson Durham Richardson Inc.,
A Joint Venture (Architects-ZGF/Engineers-HDR)

ZGF Team:
R. Doss Mabe, Ted A. Hyman, Dusty Rhoads, Stuart Baur, James Woolum, Debbie Munson, Jeffrey Daiker

HDR Team:
Randy Niehaus, Chip Warren, Dan Hahn, Gino Rapagna, Bill Kallmer

General Contractor
Hensel Phelps Construction Company:
Brian Brown, Richard Watson,
Chris Chacon, Robert Cruz

Construction Manager
Gilbane Building Company:
Robert Harper, Larry Nelson

Laboratory Planner
Earl Walls Associates

Fire Protection
Rolf Jensen & Associates

Cost Estimator
Hanscomb Associates

Photography
Nick Merrick / Hedrich Blessing Photographers, all photos unless otherwise specified; Adrian Velicescu / Standard, cover and pages 2-3, 23, 38-39, 51, 52, 58, 59, 64; Pete Eckert / Eckert & Eckert, pages 30, 88, 99, 100.

Copyright © 2005
By Edizioni Press, Inc. All rights
reserved. No part of this book may
be reproduced in any form without
written permission of the copyright
owners. All images in this book
have been reproduced with the
consent of the artists concerned
and no responsibility is accepted
by producer, publisher, or printer
for any infringement of copyright or
otherwise, arising from the contents
of this publication. Every effort has
been made to ensure that credits
comply with information supplied.

First published in the
United States of America by
Edizioni Press, Inc.
469 West 21st Street
New York, New York 10011
www.edizionipress.com

ISBN: 1-931536-30-9

Library of Congress Catalogue
Card Number: 2005927266

Printed in China

Editor
Sarah Palmer

Editorial Assistant
Nancy Sul

Design
Pure+Applied